LIGHTING
in the Domestic Interior

Renaissance to Art Nouveau

1

LIGHTING
in the Domestic Interior

Renaissance to Art Nouveau

Jonathan Bourne and Vanessa Brett

SOTHEBY'S

3

1 Design for wall-sconce
Italian, *c*1750–60
Luigi Valadier (see no.254)
(*Artemis Fine Art*)

Frontispiece
2 A girl reading a letter by lamp-light
William Henry Hunt (1790–1864), dated 1827

3 Detail of a tapestry of a banqueting scene, possibly the Twelfth Night
feast Brussels, early 17th century
With Brussels factory mark and maker's mark P.V.R.
Probably depicting January from a series of the Months of the Year.
   The room has a single sconce over the chimney-piece and also a
single candlestick on a shelf in what was obviously a fairly permanent
position, as the smoke-dome is hanging on a chain from a hook above.

4 A green-glazed stoneware lamp
Chinese, late 6th century
21cm (8¼in)
No other lamp of this exact form is recorded and it is not known
whether it was originally intended for domestic use or had some
religious significance. Jars with similar applied lotus decoration have
been found in a tomb in Hebei province, thought to date from the
560s, and a similar angular tray base features on an incense-burner from
a tomb in Henan dated to AD 595.

© 1991 Jonathan Bourne and Vanessa Brett

First published in 1991 for
Sotheby's Publications
by Philip Wilson Publishers Limited
26 Litchfield Street
London WC2H 9NJ

ISBN 0 85667 397 8
LC 91-060248

Designed by Andrew Shoolbred
Printed and bound by Singapore National Printers Ltd, Singapore

Contents

4

Preface

This book is a pictorial survey of domestic lighting in Europe and North America. It is neither a detailed study of the science of lighting nor a comprehensive look at the designs and styles used by craftsmen: to attempt such massive tasks would have been beyond our brief and take longer than our schedule permitted. We have attempted a broad coverage of the many materials and methods used but have concentrated on the finer examples produced by, or under the direction of, some of the best artists and craftsmen in over six hundred years.

We hope readers will find interesting the many questions of design, technique, and relationships between crafts that juxtapositions of illustrations raise. We hope, too, that they will enjoy the apparently limitless imagination of the creators of these objects – be they beautiful, utilitarian, amusing or fantastic.

Electricity is so much a part of twentieth-century living that we rarely think of what life was like for previous generations. The provision of artificial light, through oil, candles and gas, was both time consuming and expensive. We must all be grateful for the inventiveness of those who strove to improve the science of lighting, whose work we take so much for granted today.

I believe that men are generally still a little afraid of the
dark, though the witches are all hung, and Christianity and
candles have been introduced.

HENRY DAVID THOREAU

5 The Connoisseur
Desflaches, mid-19th century

6 The central panel of a Gobelins tapestry depicting 'Don Quixote at the ball given for him in Barcelona by Don Antonio' French, dated 1758 and signed: Cozette; the design for the panel by Coypel

6

Introduction

It is almost impossible for us, living in our hundred-watt age, to imagine how little light there was in houses after dark, certainly until the advent of gaslight in the nineteenth century. The strongest light in a room would often come from the fire which, as a source of both heat and light, was very much the focal point of a room. Methods of lighting did not change very much until the middle of the nineteenth century. Good wax candles were expensive; oil lamps, tallow candles and rushlights were often smelly and smoky and, in the case of the last two, all too quickly consumed.

Lives were ruled by the hours of daylight and people tended to rise earlier than today, eat at very different times (the main meal of the day being in the middle of the afternoon), and go to bed earlier. The number of candles a person was willing to burn after dark was a sure indication of his or her wealth, and a room opulently lit was certain to arouse comment and gossip. For the poor the day started at sunrise and ended at sunset.

A small room in a grand house would usually have had one central chandelier, maybe some candelabra and then candlesticks which could be brought in and moved around at will. A larger room, at least in the seventeenth and early eighteenth centuries, would have had several smaller chandeliers rather than one large one. One or two people on their own after dark would probably have used no more than two candlesticks to illuminate their activities or maybe, by the latter half of the eighteenth century, a candle lamp. It is noticeable how little lighting apparatus appears in contemporary paintings.

Today our eyes are used to the flat glare of the electric bulb. Candle flames and, to a lesser extent, oil lights, flickered and moved, imbuing objects in a room with shadow and movement. Carved decoration was thrown into greater relief and polished surfaces – gilding, silver, looking-glasses – glowed; all objects seemed to have a life of their own.

The holders for candles and oil became more and more elaborate through the centuries. Oil lamps took on bizarre forms in the sixteenth century in Italy and candle-holders became more sophisticated in the late seventeenth century and into the eighteenth century. Reflecting surfaces, polished silver and brass, mirror-plates and rock-crystal or glass, were utilized as much as possible to enhance the light power of candle-holders. There are basically three types of candle-holder: the candlestick or candelabra (to stand on a flat surface), the sconce or wall-light (to be fixed to a wall), and the chandelier or lantern (which hangs from the ceiling). There were of course many variations to these basic themes and they were adapted for oil and gas in the nineteenth century. Terms crop up in inventories that are difficult now to understand – what, for instance, were the 'chandeliers à la financière' which appear in Cardinal Mazarin's inventories? Probably they were specially suited for office work rather than being favoured by bankers.

At the end of the eighteenth century oil lighting took several leaps forward in efficiency and once again became popular. Through the nineteenth century oil lamps were usually brought into a room as darkness fell, having been cleaned and re-filled in domestic quarters, though sometimes they appear, from contemporary pictures, to have been left standing in a room throughout the daylight hours.

It was only with the advent of gas lighting that lives took on more the pattern that we know today. The source of power was on tap with no great expense of effort and gave a strong, more regular light. Finally, electricity gave us the cleanliness and efficiency we know today.

She may very well pass for forty-three
In the dark with a light behind her.

W.S. GILBERT, *Trial by Jury*

7 Le Minuit
French engraving, early 19th century
Showing a young lady preparing for bed
before her dressing table, which has attached
candle-branches.

(Private collection)

8

7

8

8 A scene, possibly a wedding, in a Venetian palace
Attributed to Paolo Fiammingo (1540?–96)
The elaborately decorated lantern hanging from the ceiling was possibly made of metal, but more likely of carved wood, gilded and painted. It probably only contained a single candle which cannot have shed a great deal of light.

9

9 A masked ball
Veronese school, mid-18th century

10 Tax collectors
Marinus von Reymerswael
(see no. 29)

10

At our request the anchorite hunted among his piles of
rubbish with a candlestick covered with the thick grease of
years, trying unsuccessfully to find one of his shorthand
pamphlets in print.

Diary of the Revd Francis Kilvert, 3 July 1872

The earliest oil lights were made of stone by Palaeolithic man. The stone was hollowed out and a small groove was cut at one side to take the wick of bark or fibre. N. Ault in *Life in Ancient Britain* suggests that lamps of this kind were certainly in use in 15,000 BC and a Moravian lamp has been dated at 30,000 years old. Stone lamps from 4,000 BC have been found in Cyprus and some finely decorated examples, often with stands, have been dated to 1,500 BC.

In coastal areas shells were used and these have been found in Ur, Mesopotamia and in many locations around the Mediterranean. Scallop, whelk and oyster shells were widely used, often fuelled by fish oil.

Gradually lamps of other materials began to be made, sometimes in the form of shells. In the East alabaster was used. Pottery lamps have been excavated all over the ancient world and, less widely, examples made of bronze. The open bowl or saucer lamp was a development of the hollowed stone. Herodotus (*c*485–425 BC) writes of the 'Festival of Lamps' in which saucer-shaped lamps were filled with a mixture of castor oil and salt, upon which the wick floated. Ancient Chinese lamps are also found using the floating wick method. Throughout the Pacific, halved coconut shells were used as saucer lamps, and in Brazil nut oil was used as fuel.

11

11 Lamp made from hollowed-out stone
(Trustees of the Science Museum, London)

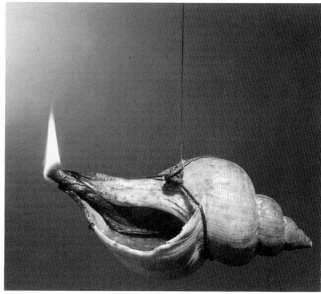

12

12 Lamp made from a conch shell
(Trustees of the Science Museum, London)

The Greeks were the first to curve the rim of the saucer lamps inwards and cover the nozzles to form a spout. The Romans developed this form and often manufactured highly decorated examples in pottery or bronze (no.14). Often the lamps had more than one spout – one lamp found in Pompeii[1] had fourteen – and were suspended from the ceiling or a stand by chains.

13 Study of a Roman lamp-stand
Gabriel Auguste Ancelet
(1829–95)

14 Engraving of a group of antique oil lamps
Giovanni Battista Piranesi
(1720–78)
From the set of 110 plates produced between 1768 and 1778 and published in Rome in 1778 as *Vasi, candelabri, cippi, sarcofagi, tripodi, lucerne ed ornamenti antichi*

(Private collection)

Then shall the kingdom of heaven be likened unto ten virgins, which took their lamps and went forth to meet the bridegroom; and five of them were wise and five were foolish. They that were foolish took their lamps, and took no oil in them: but the wise took oil in their vessels with their lamps. While the bridegroom tarried, they all slumbered and slept. And at midnight there was a cry made, Behold, the bridegroom cometh, go ye out to meet him. Then all those virgins arose, and trimmed their lamps. And the foolish said unto the wise, Give us of your oil; for our lamps are gone out. But the wise answered, saying, Not so; lest there be not enough for us and you: but go ye rather to them that sell and buy for yourselves.

MATTHEW 25 v1–8

[1] Now in the Naples Museum. Another with at least sixteen lights and more elaborately decorated is in the Etruscan Academy Museum, Casali House, Piazza Signorelli, Cortona

15

16

15 A bronze oil lamp
Italian, late 15th/early 16th century
7cm (2¾in)
The silver eyes and naturalistically chased hair make this an apparently
unique example of the more commonly known type of Paduan oil lamp,
intended to imitate the Antique.

16 A bronze hanging oil lamp
Northern Italy, probably Mantua, *c*1500
14cm (5½in)
In the form of an acrobat with silver eyes. This lamp must always have
been intended to amuse whoever it was shedding light upon, who was
presumably to infer that it was the acrobat's gassy emissions that kept
the flame burning brightly, rather than the reservoir of oil.

This belongs to a group of somewhat similar suspended and standing
lamps which have been historically attributed to the Riccio workshop at
Padua, but the silver eyes seem much closer to work produced in
Mantua, inspired by Antico's work for the Gonzaga court. Though
obviously classical in inspiration, there is no recorded prototype for this
model.

There was very little advancement in the style or technique of lamps from Roman to mediaeval times. Most were made of earthenware or iron and have consequently not survived. Only in Italy, it seems, did oil lamps assume fantastic shapes and follow weird designs often based on antique originals.

17 Two bronze lamps
Padua, *c*1500
14cm and 13cm (5½in and 5in) long
Other lamps of this same basic form are recorded, and indeed the idea of a grotesque creature forming a lamp seemed a popular one during the Renaissance. These creatures proliferate also in decorative designs for other metalwork, as well as architecture and furniture, and were thought to be in an antique style then popular.

18 A bronze oil lamp
Italian, possibly Padua, *c*1500
21cm (8¼in)
In the form of a dragonesque satyr supported on lion's legs at the front and his dolphin-like tail. The hollow body has two compartments, the lower with an opening between the creature's knees and with a conduit for the wick. An engraving of the present lamp was illustrated in *L'Antiquité expliquée* by Bernard de Montfaucon, published in Paris as early as 1722 (see no.18a).[2] It was at one time thought to be by the celebrated sculptor Andrea Riccio.

[2] Vol.V, pl.CXLVI; at which time the lamp was in the collection of one R.P. Albert

17

18a

18

The candle, along with the oil lamp, is man's oldest efficient answer to the problem of supplying light after dark. The principle of a fibre wick surrounded by a solid inflammable substance was certainly known in Egypt and Crete as early as 3,000 BC, and it was probably the Romans who disseminated its use throughout Europe. From that time until the second quarter of the nineteenth century, the candle was the most widely used form of artificial lighting. In mediaeval times it is doubtful if candles were much in use outside the great houses, churches and monasteries, but by the sixteenth century, a period remarkable for the rise in living standards of the poorer people, candlesticks appear more regularly in household inventories.

Candles for everyday use were made of tallow or purified animal fat. Mutton tallow was the best, then beef; occasionally pig's fat was used, though this produced a smelly black smoke. In farming districts candles were often made at home, probably by the women of the household. This was forbidden in England after 1709, by Act of Parliament, and candles had to be bought; however, sometimes a farmer produced candles for local people. The slaughter of one bullock would provide enough tallow for all the candles used on an average farm for three years. In remote areas candles continued to be made at home: while visiting the Isle of Coll, in the Hebrides, in 1773, Samuel Johnson saw candles being made in almost every house.

In London both the wax chandlers and tallow chandlers had formed their guilds before the end of the fifteenth century. Every market town, and some villages also, had at least one chandler or candle-maker. Nearby farms and slaughter-houses would provide their raw materials and nearly all of them undertook the unsavoury task of rendering tallow.

A large cauldron was used for the melting down of the fat, from which impurities were first skimmed when they rose to the surface. Water was then added to separate the last waste material, which settled in a layer between the water and fat. This residue was then pressed to extract any remaining tallow and the resulting cakey substance, known as greave, was fed to dogs, pigs and even ducks. The wick was made by twisting several strands of spun cotton together, which was then cut to the desired length and pulled tight to remove knots which might cause spluttering.

The cheapest candles were known as dips, after the method of manufacture. The chandler suspended a number of wicks from a rod, known as a broach, and holding this at each end, immersed the wicks in a small bath of molten tallow. The wicks were raised coated with a thin layer of tallow and then left to harden before re-immersion to retain a further coating. This operation was repeated until the candles had achieved the desired thickness. The pointed base-ends were removed by passing them over a hot brass plate.

Beeswax candles were far superior to those made of tallow – they smoked less, burned brighter, and did not give off the unpleasant smell of tallow candles. The method of manufacture was completely different from tallow candles. The wax was

19 Interior of a kitchen
Pieter van der Heyden, after
Hieronymus Bosch, dated 1567
Two forms of lighting can be seen
in this busy kitchen scene: a
bracket containing a single candle
fixed to the front of the fireplace
and an oil lamp hanging
immediately below it.

(Christopher Mendez Ltd)

melted and strained to remove the impurities, and then the very yellow product was laid in strips in the sun to be bleached. The wax was then melted in a cauldron and ladled onto the wicks, suspended from a sort of iron hoop above. While still warm and soft the candles were then rolled into shape with hardwood rollers, which had to be kept moist to avoid the candles sticking to them.

20 A bronze pricket candlestick
German, 2nd half 12th century
32.5cm (5½in)

21 A gilded copper and champlevé enamel travelling candlestick
Limoges, 13th century
23cm (9in)

22 A copper and enamel pricket candlestick
Limoges, early 14th century
18.4cm (7¼in)
The pricket is hollow, resting on an hexagonal base decorated with red, green and blue champlevé enamel; there are traces of the original gilding.

20

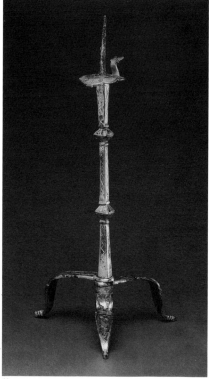

21

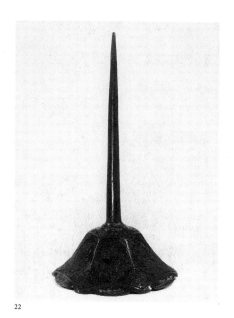

22

The simplest form of candle was the rushlight, usually made by drawing a rush through kitchen fat, and these were used widely wherever the common soft rush (*Juncus effusus*) was found. John Aubrey reported in 1673 that the inhabitants of Ockley in Surrey made their own lights from rushes, and the Revd Gilbert White describes their manufacture in detail.[3] They remained in use in parts of Wales well into the present century.

The rushes were collected in late summer when they were fully grown but still green. The tops were cut off and the outer skin peeled off, leaving a single strip of skin supporting the pith roughly eighteen inches in length. These strips were left to dry and then carefully drawn through fat heated in a special boat-shaped pan called a grisset. The rushes were then left to dry once more, before being burnt in specially made holders (nos 23–24). The jaws of the holder clamped the rush at roughly a 45 degree angle and about 1½ inches was drawn through at a time, taking about twenty minutes to burn a whole rush. The holders were never mass produced, but individually made by local blacksmiths.

In England rushlights were excluded from the Act of Parliament of 1709 which imposed a tax and partial ban on the making of candles, and were by far the cheapest form of lighting. Later in the eighteenth century and in the nineteenth century agricultural labourers became increasingly impoverished and were unable to afford meat more than once a week; they therefore had little excess fat to make rushlights, forcing them to buy the more expensive candles and thus increasing their penury.

The next day commenced as before, getting up and dressing by rushlight....

CHARLOTTE BRONTË, *Jane Eyre*, 1847

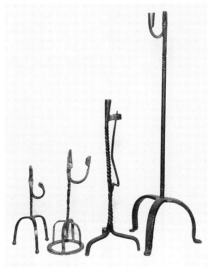

23 Iron rushlight and candle-holders
16th/17th century
27.3cm to 82cm (32in to 10¾in)

24 Rushlight in use

(Trustees of the Science Museum, London)

[3] *Natural History of Selborne*, 1775

23

24

measure, brought me up. She used to get the meadow-rushes, such as they tie the hop-shoots to the poles with. She cut them when they had attained their full substance, but were still green. The rush, at this age, consists of a body of pith with a green skin on it. You cut off both ends of the rush, and leave the prime part, which, on an average, may be about a foot and half long. Then you take off all the green skin, except for about a fifth part of the way round the pith. Thus it is a piece of pith, all but a little strip of skin in one part, all the way up, which, observe, is necessary to hold the pith together all the way along.

The rushes being thus prepared, the grease is melted, and put in a melted state into something that is as long as the rushes are. The rushes are put into the grease; soaked in it sufficiently; then taken out and laid in a bit of bark taken from a young tree, so as not to be too large. This bark is fixed up against the wall by a couple of straps put round it; and there it hangs for the purpose of holding the rushes.

The rushes are carried about in the hand; but to sit by, to work by, or to go to bed by, they are fixed in stands made for the purpose, some of which are high, to stand on the ground, and some low, to stand on a table. The stands have an iron port something like a pair of pliers to hold the rush in, and the rush is shifted forward from time to time, as it burns down to the thing that holds it.

Now these rushes give a better light than a common small dip-candle; and they cost next to nothing, though the labourer may with them have as much light as he pleases, and though without them he must sit the far greater part of the winter evenings in the dark, even if he expend fifteen shillings a year in candles. You may do any sort of work by this light; and, if reading be your taste, you may read the foul libels, the lies and abuse, which are circulated gratis about me by the 'Society for Promoting Christian Knowledge', as well by rush-light as you can by the light of taxed candles; and at any rate, you would have one less evil; for to be deceived and to pay a tax for the deception are a little too much for even modern loyalty openly to demand.

WILLIAM COBBETT, *Cottage Economy*, 1821

We are not permitted to make candles ourselves, and if we were, they ought seldom to be used in a labourer's family. I was bred and brought up mostly by rush-light, and I do not find that I see less clearly than other people. Candles certainly were not much used in English labourers' dwellings in the days when they had meat dinners and Sunday coats. Potatoes and taxed candles seem to have grown into fashion together; and, perhaps, for this reason: that when the pot ceased to afford grease for the rushes, the potato-gorger was compelled to go to the chandler's shop for light to swallow the potatoes by, else he might have devoured peeling and all!

My grandmother, who lived to be pretty nearly ninety, never, I believe, burnt a candle in her house in her life. I know that I never saw one there, and she, in a great

25

26

27

28

25 A bronze candlestick
Probably Flemish, *c*1550
12cm (4¾in)
This is a rare form, having a very short stem and wide base. A similar example was found in the wreck of the *Mary Rose*, Henry VIII's warship which sank in 1545 off Portsmouth.

(Peter Hornsby)

26 A maiolica candlestick
Italian (Gubbio), mid-16th century
12.7cm (5in)

(Trustees of the Victoria & Albert Museum, London)

27 A latten candlestick
Flemish, early 16th century
14cm (5½in)

28 Two brass candlesticks
Flemish, 16th century
This photograph shows the difference in colour and patina that can be found in brassware: the result of variation in the alloys and different methods of cleaning and restoration.
   The design of the sconces shows the large rectangular hole seen on early candlesticks, allowing the candle stub to be eased out.

(Peter Hornsby)

29 Tax collectors
Marinus von Reymerswael
Detail of the painting on p.11, showing a candlestick in brass, typical of the period, with a pair of snuffers lying on the base.

30 A brass pricket candlestick
Flemish, mid-15th century
49cm (19¼in)

29

30

Superior to the dip method of manufacture were mould candles. These are believed to have originated in France in the fifteenth century. Certainly by the early seventeenth century candle moulds figure quite widely in contemporary inventories. The mould gave the candle a more regular finish than was possible with the dip method and better quality tallow had to be used, as the cheaper sort was too sticky for use in the moulds. The moulds were usually made by pewterers and took the form of a number of cylinders with conical ends set in a trough supported by a frame. It was important to keep the wicks tightly stretched while the hot tallow was added.

31 Design for a candlestick
Italian, *c*1540
After Giulio Romano
Giulio Gianuzzi (?1492–1546), known as Giulio Romano, an influential painter and architect in the Mannerist style who worked for the Gonzagas at Mantua and designed buildings, tapestries and metalwork. No objects based directly on his designs are known to survive.

(Trustees of the Victoria & Albert Museum, London)

32 Design for a candlestick
Erasmus Hornick
Hornick (d.1583), Flemish goldsmith and designer in the most extravagant Mannerist style, worked with Jamnitzer in Nuremberg and, towards the end of his life, became 'Kammergoldschmied' to the greatest Mannerist patron, Emperor Rudolph II, in Prague.

(Trustees of the Victoria & Albert Museum, London)

33 A bronze candlestick
Venetian, early 16th century
28.5cm (11¼in)
A similar pair in the Victoria & Albert Museum is attributed to the workshop of Alessandro Leopardi.

34 A pottery candlestick
French (St Porchaire), mid-16th century
There has long been considerable mystery about the extremely elaborate pottery confections, often with French Royal insignia, which have been attributed since the late 1880s to St Porchaire. Only a few (between sixty and seventy) items are recorded and, although the factory was active before 1540, the more elaborate pieces probably date from the middle of the century. None of these appear in early inventories, and they were, for a long time, thought to be 19th-century creations (see no.699).

(Trustees of the Victoria & Albert Museum, London)

31

32

33

34

35

35 Chandelier in the form of a dragon
Nuremberg, 1522
William Stoss after Albrecht Dürer

(Germanisches Nationalmuseum, Nuremberg)

36 Watercolour of a chandelier
F.E. Assman, Inscribed: Chandelier in the
Museum of the Green Vaults, Dresden
German, late 15th/early 16th century

(Trustees of the Victoria & Albert Museum, London)

36

37 Design for a chandelier
Italian, *c*1585
Jacopo Ligozzi
Perhaps designed by Ligozzi
(1547–1626) for the marriage
festivities of Cesare d'Este and
Virginia Medici at Florence in
1585.

*(Trustees of the Victoria & Albert
Museum, London)*

38 Design for a chandelier
René Boyvin (*c*1525–98)
Boyvin worked in Paris, where he
produced a large number of
engravings after the work of
masters such as Giulio Romano,
but principally those of the
Fontainebleau school, notably
Rosso Fiorentino.

(Private collection)

37

38

Nos 39–47 show the spread of a particular style among craftsmen working in various media and in different countries. The domed base, rising to a drip-pan and vase or cylindrical-shaped sconce is found from the mid-sixteenth to the late seventeenth century. The form appears first in Italy, then spreads north to Germany, France and England. In some areas modified versions of the style were still being made in the nineteenth century – for example by pewterers in Spain and Portugal.[4]

39 A gilded bronze candlestick
Venetian, early 16th century
18cm (7in)

40 A bronze candlestick
Italian (probably Venetian), early 17th century
14.6cm (5¾in)

41 Design for a candlestick and snuffer
German, *c*1560
Erasmus Hornick
Hornick made many designs for goldsmiths. He worked in Augsburg, Nuremberg and lastly in Prague for Rudolph II.

(Trustees of the Victoria & Albert Museum, London)

42 A silver candlestick
South German, *c*1590–1600
18.6cm (7¼in); 17.8cm (7in)
This is one of a pair of candlesticks which differ slightly, probably indicating that they were once part of a larger set, made and decorated by different craftsmen using the same design source. Very few 16th-century silver candlesticks survive, but the type is well known in bronze and brass, many of Venetian origin, as can be seen in no.39.

Engraved with contemporary armorials dated 1590 and 1601: of Thun for Johann Anton von Thun (*c*1559–1602), Dean of Salzburg Catnedral, and of von Schroffenstein, for his mother.

(Now in the Thyssen-Bornemisza collection)[5]

41

39

40

42

[4] For illustrations, see Peter Hornsby, *Pewter of the Western World*, Schiffer, Exton, Pennsylvania, 1983, no.1089; or Vanessa Brett, *Phaidon Guide to Pewter*, Oxford, 1981, p.139

[5] Hannelore Müller, *European Silver,* London, 1986, no. 45

43

44

45

43 A silver candlestick
Danzig, *c*1660
Andrew (Andrzej) Mackensen
21.6cm (8½in)
The engraved initials are those of
Venceslaus de Leszno
Leszczynski (1605–66), who was
appointed First Secretary to
Sigismund III, King of Poland in
1629, Secretary of the Realm in
1630 and Primate of the Realm in
1658.
    Andrew Mackensen, born
*c*1600 of Scottish parentage, was
appointed Royal Goldsmith in
Cracow in 1628 and moved to
Danzig in 1643. He died in 1670.

44 A faience candlestick 'in the
white'
German, late 17th century
20cm (7¾in)
This shape can also be seen in a
maiolica candlestick from Faenza,
1619–38, part of a service made
for Johann Georg I, Elector of
Saxony and bearing his arms.[6]

45 A glass candlestick
Late 17th century
25.5cm (10in)
Though candlesticks of this type
have been attributed to Liège, the
stem formation bears a
remarkably close resemblance to
those found on Nuremberg
goblets.

46 A brass candlestick
English, 17th century
24cm (9½in)

47 Two brass candlesticks
German, *c*1680

(Peter Hempson)

46

[6] *State Art Collections of Dresden*, exh. cat.,
Dresden, 1978

47

48

49

50

48 A bronze candlestick
Nuremberg, early 17th century
18cm (7in)

49 A pewter candlestick
English, dated 1616
William Grainger
The relief decoration on this
candlestick is found on a small
group of English 17th-century
pewter. The technique was used
more widely in Germany, where it
is known as 'Edelzinn'.

*(Trustees of the Victoria & Albert
Museum, London)*

50 A pewter candlestick
English, *c*1580–1620
21cm (8¼in)
This type is known as a 'bell'
candlestick, due to the shape of
the base.

(Private collection)

51 A brass candlestick
French, late 16th century

(Peter Hornsby)

52 A pair of pricket candlesticks
Nuremberg, *c*1580
Christoph Ritter II

(H.S. Wellby Ltd)

51

53 A silver candlestick
London, 1615
Maker's mark W.C.
12.7cm (5in)
The single candle-holder rests on
a wire-work triform base. English
silver candlesticks prior to 1650
are very rare: Michael Clayton[7]
mentions two similar examples
dated 1618.

(Brand Inglis Ltd)

52

53

54

54 Four silver candlesticks
London, 1637
Maker's mark W.G.
14cm (5½in)
This is possibly the earliest set of
English silver candlesticks to have
survived.[8]

55 Design for a candlestick
Adam van Vianen (Utrecht,
*c*1565–1627)
Adam's son, Christian, published
a book of his father's designs in
Utrecht in 1650.

(Private collection)

55

56 A silver wall-sconce
Utrecht, dated 1622
Adam van Vianen
59.8cm (23½in)
One of a pair. These are the only
wall-lights recorded by Adam van
Vianen (*c*1565–1627). Adam and
his elder brother Paul are
renowned for the skill of their
chasing and for their
development of the lobate or
auricular style. Paul eventually
settled in Prague at the court of
Rudolf II, where he died in 1613,
whereas Adam remained in their
native Utrecht. Many of Adam's
designs were published in 1650
by his son, Christian (also a
silversmith) (see no.55).
   The mythological scenes on
these sconces are found on other
objects by Paul: the larger,
representing Syrinx changed into
reeds, pursued by Pan and
watched by nymphs (illustrated
here) and Diana and Actaeon, are
on two plaques by Paul dated
1612 and 1613,[9] whilst the
smaller plaques show Mercury
holding the head of Argus
(illustrated) and a stag-hunting
scene.

56

[7] *The Collector's Dictionary of the Silver and Gold of Great Britain and North America*, London,
1971, p.37

[8] For the only known example of the style in pewter, see *Pewter, A celebration of the craft
1200–1700*, exh. cat., The Museum of London, 1989, no.51

[9] In the Centraal Museum, Utrecht, ill.in *De Utrechtse edelsmeden Van Vianen*, exh. cat.,
Utrecht, 1984, nos 30/31

The second half of the seventeenth century, during which period nos 57–61 & 66 were made, is considered by collectors to be the greatest period for English pewter, however this may simply reflect the fact that it is the earliest period from which a considerable quantity of pewter has survived. Pewter is an alloy of tin and, as with silver, it was common to trade in worn-out or unfashionable objects, so that they could be melted for re-use. Because of its comparative rarity today, it is hard to appreciate how widely pewter was used. Although too expensive for many households, it was nonetheless considerably cheaper than silver.[10]

57

58

59

60

61

62

57 A pewter candlestick
English, mid-17th century
23.5cm (9¼in)
One of a pair, this is a particularly fine example of a style that is rare in pewter. It is engraved with unidentified contemporary armorials.

(The Worshipful Company of Pewterers)

58 A pewter candlestick
English, mid-17th century
16cm (6¼in)
This is the only recorded example of this form of candlestick (without a drip-pan) in pewter; similar examples are known in brass however.

(Private collection)

59 A brass candlestick
English, c1650
Candlesticks of this form (see also no.57) are commonly called 'trumpet based', purely because of their shape. The ridged decoration seen here on the stem and on no.60 was popular with brassworkers and pewterers. The wide drip-pan seen also on nos 57 and 64 had a functional purpose as tallow candles dripped excessively. By the 18th century, when wax candles were more commonly used, the drip-pan disappeared from the design. An example of a trumpet-based candlestick in silver, dated 1663, embossed with foliage, is in the Kremlin Museum, Moscow.[11]

(Peter Hornsby)

60 A pewter candlestick
English, c1670
16cm (6¼in)
(Private collection)

61 A pewter candlestick
English, c1680–90
15cm (6in)
(Private collection)

62 A brass candlestick
Spanish or Dutch, 17th century
The form of this candlestick is typically Spanish, but it may be that it was made in Holland for export to Spain.

(Peter Hornsby)

[10] See *Pewter, A celebration of the craft, 1200–1700*, exh. cat., The Museum of London, 1989

[11] Ill. pl.59B in Charles Oman, *Caroline Silver*, London, 1970

63 Detail from a painting of
elegant company in an interior
Simon de Vos (1603–76,
Antwerp)
An unlit candle in an elaborately
turned candlestick is on the table.

64 A brass candlestick
Dutch, c1700
This design of candlestick was
popular in the Low Countries in
the 17th and early 18th centuries.
The form is sometimes known as
'Heemskerk' after a group of
candlesticks found in the wreck of
an expedition which foundered at
the island of Novaya Zemlya in
1596, whose captain was
Heemskerk.[12]

(Peter Hornsby)

65 Two pairs of silver
candlesticks
Spanish, c1600
One: Antonio Perez, Toledo; the
other unmarked

(Brand Inglis Ltd)

63

64

65

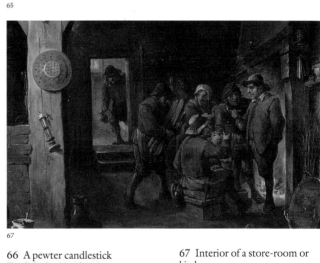

67

66

66 A pewter candlestick
English, 2nd half 17th century
24.5cm (9¾in)

*(The Worshipful Company of Pewterers,
London)*

67 Interior of a store-room or
kitchen
David Teniers the Younger, dated
1681
Showing what is probably a base-
metal candlestick hanging from
one of the posts, ready to be
taken down and used.

[12] Now in the Rijksmuseum, Amsterdam

68

69a

69

68 An interior with elegant
company
Dirck Hals
The brass chandelier is typical of
the period and many in this style
were produced in the Low
Countries, Germany, France and
England.

69 A brass chandelier
German, mid-17th century
152cm (5ft)
Two of the branches marked: W.
Pfenings 1 & 2 and P. Plum

70 A tin lantern
18th/19th century, probably
American
Of a type that changed little from
the 17th to the 19th century.

(J.W. Blum collection)

71 Girl at a window, about to
light a lantern from a candle-flame
Gerard (Gerrit) Dou (1613–75)

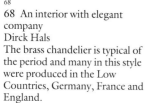

70

71

The oil lamp had still not appreciably advanced since ancient times. Crusie lamps were of Celtic origin and often double-bowled, though only with a single wick, the lower bowl or dish being merely to catch the drips. They were extensively used throughout Britain and in the Channel Islands were known as croiset or crasset lamps. They gave rise to certain superstitions – a blue flame meant wind the next day, a green flame denoted the presence of a witch and a spark meant news coming to the person in whose direction the spark flew.

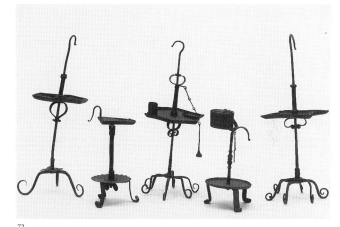

72 A group of wrought-iron pan lights and crusie lamps
German, 17th century
26cm to 43cm (10¼in to 17in)

73 Woman contemplating a skull by the light of a simple double-spouted oil lamp
Andreani

(Christopher Mendez Ltd)

73

72

74

74 Still-life with an oil lamp
Gotthardt de Wedig
(1583–1641)

75 Interior of a kitchen
Cornelis Visscher (?1629–58)
The etching depicts a kitchen by day, with various forms of lighting in readiness for use: a candlestick by the window, an outside lamp or lantern on the shelving above the seated figures, and an oil lamp by the fireside, probably of the type shown in the still-life of no.74.

(Christopher Mendez Ltd)

75

Nos 76–82 and 88–90 show the popularity of one style among goldsmiths of different countries. The column candlestick, made in a variety of materials (pewter, brass, treen and ceramics) was popular in the last quarter of the seventeenth century, then went out of favour until the 1760s (nos 402–7).

76 A silver candlestick
Paris, 1664
Pierre Masse
17.4cm (6¾in)
Pierre Masse is thought to have been a specialist maker of candlesticks, who became a master in 1639. See also no.85

(Now in the Thyssen-Bornemisza collection; formerly in the Mentmore collection)

77 A silver candlestick
French (Clermont-Ferrand), *c*1687
Antoine Vassadel
17.3cm (6¾in)
Very little French silver from the period of Louis XIV has survived, chiefly due to the melting of plate in 1689 and 1709.

78 A silver candlestick
London, 1669
Jacob Bodendick
31.1cm (12¼in)
Bodendick, who came to work in London from Limburg in Germany, made some of the finest cast and embossed work of his time. In 1664, together with Wolfgang Howzer (from Zurich) he presented a letter from Charles II to the Wardens of the Goldsmiths' Company, instructing them to assay and mark their work.[13] Several candlesticks by Bodendick have survived (see also no.86) and among his other work are notable tankards and cagework cups.

This candlestick is very similar to another by the same maker of 1667,[14] made of thin-gauge sheet silver. Their design shows how closely Bodendick worked to his native German style.

79 A pair of silver candlesticks
Augsburg, *c*1680

(H.S. Wellby Ltd)

80 A pair of silver candlesticks
London, 1693
Maker's mark R.S.
20.3cm (8in)

(Brand Inglis Ltd)

81 A pair of silver candlesticks
German (Kassel), *c*1690

(H.S. Wellby Ltd)

76

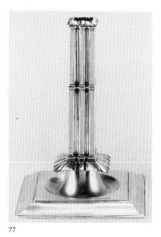

77

78

79

80

81

82

82 A pair of brass candlesticks
French, *c*1680
The circular cluster column form
is rare in brass. An English
example without a drip-pan is in
Winterthur Museum.[15]

(Peter Hempson)

83 A silver candlestick
London, 1692
Maker's mark T.B.
28.5cm (11¼in)

84 A pair of brass candlesticks
Scandinavian, *c*1670
These are made of sheet brass,
decorated with repoussé, rather
than being cast.

(Peter Hempson)

85 A silver-gilt dressing table
candlestick
Paris, 1661–63
Pierre Masse
This candlestick is part of the
renowned Lennoxlove toilet
service, found in a disused room
in the mediaeval tower at
Lennoxlove, near Edinburgh in
1900. It is thought to have been
owned originally by Frances
Teresa Stuart, Duchess of
Richmond and Lennox
(1647–1702). Samuel Pepys
described her as 'the beautifullest
creature that ever I did see in my
life'. The service comprises
seventeen pieces of silver-gilt,
contained in sixteen leather-
covered cases and stored in its
original walnut-veneered chest.
It was completed by 1677.[16]

*(Now in the Scottish National Museum,
Edinburgh)*

86 A silver-gilt candlestick
English, *c*1665
Jacob Bodendick (maker's mark
only)
24.8cm (9¾in)

83

84

85

86

... What say you to the good example set by the King who
has had his finest silver melted down? Our Duchesse du
Lude is in despair but feels obliged to follow suit; Mme de
Chaulnes has given her ornamental tables, Mme de
Lavardin her silver service which came from Rome, in the
belief her husband will not be recalled there; pray look into
your affairs and see if you can contribute in any way ...

LETTER FROM MADAME DE SÉVIGNÉ, dated 18 December 1689

[13] Philippa Glanville, *Silver in England*, London, 1987, p.232

[14] Sotheby's, London, 19 November 1987, lot 41

[15] Ill. in Rupert Gentle and Rachael Feild, *English Domestic Brass*, London, 1975, p. 110, fig.6

[16] Godfrey Evans, 'The Lennoxlove Toilet Service', International Silver and Jewellery Fair,
London, 1990; and Godfrey Evans, 'Saved from the Melting Pot', *Country Life*, 9 March 1989

87 A pair of silver toilet candlesticks
Paris, 1665
10.8cm (4¼in)

88
Two silver-gilt candlesticks
London
One: Robert Smythier, 1670; the other:
maker's mark I.H. a fleur-de-lys and pellets
below, 1676
17cm (6¾in)
Robert Smythier (free in 1660) worked
extensively for the Jewel House. Charles
Oman[17] wrote 'Probably more plate has
survived bearing the mark S crowned than any
other used in the reign of Charles II'. (see also
no.98) The maker I.H. is also known for the
fine quality of his work, notably tankards, but
his identity is unknown. A pair of very similar
candlesticks with the maker's mark W.H.[18]
raises the question of the extent to which this
generation of silversmiths, many not born in
England, collaborated in their work.

89 A parcel-gilt silver candlestick
Hamburg, 1670-75
Nicolas Feindt I
33.8cm (13¼in)

90 A pair of grisaille enamel candlesticks
Limoges, c1675
Signed: Jacques I. Laudin
26cm (10in)
Bearing the arms of Henri de Daillon, comte
de Lude, born about 1623.

[17] Charles Oman, *Caroline Silver*, London,
1970, p.31

[18] Christie's, London, 27 April 1983

87

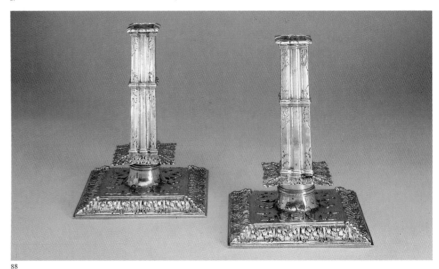

88

89

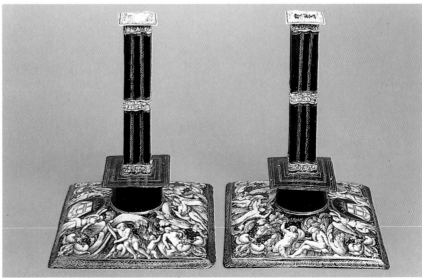

90

To White Hall; and Mr. Pierce showed me
the Queene's bedchamber, and her closet,
where she had nothing but some pretty pious
pictures, and books of devotion; and her holy
water at her head as she sleeps, with a clock by
her bed-side, wherein a lamp burns that tells
her the time of the night at any time.

DIARY OF SAMUEL PEPYS, 24 June 1664

91 An ebonized night clock
English, c1665
77cm (30¼in)
This is a rare English version of a
type of clock which was more
popular in Italy. The interior is
fitted with a space for a candle,
which lights the painted panel
from behind, shedding a gentle
comforting light throughout the
night and also making it possible
to tell the time without lighting a
candle. The introduction of
repeating mechanisms in clocks in
the 1670s made night clocks
redundant.

91

92 A woman reading by candle-
light
Frans van Mieris the elder
(1635–81, Leiden), *c*1665
Frans van Mieris was apprenticed
to Gerard Dou, famous for his
genre painting. The drawing is in
black chalk on vellum, though it
does not appear to be a sketch for
one of the numerous candle-light
scenes by van Mieris.

(Artemis Fine Art)

92

93 Student at a table by candle-
light
Rembrandt Harmensz van Rijn
(1606–69)
This etching shows the subdued
light that was common in the
17th and 18th centuries. Most of
the room is in shadow, with one
candle giving just enough light
for the student to read by.

93

94 An interior with a family
Quiringh Gerritsz van
Brekelenkam (*c*1620–68)
A rather more prosperous interior
also has a candle-holder, this time
in brass, fixed to the wall and near
the chimney-piece, as we have
seen before, see no.19.

95 A bronze wall-sconce
English, *c*1685
18cm (7in)
The idea of the outstretched arm
holding a light was a popular one
and can be found in several
media. Peter Thornton
(*Seventeenth century Interior
Decoration in England, France
and Holland*) illustrates several
in situ. An English silver sconce,
using a similar motif of a rosette is
in the Victoria & Albert
Museum.[19]

(Brand Inglis Ltd)

96 A brass wall-sconce
Dutch, 17th century, dated 1681

(Peter Hornsby)

97 A brass wall-light
Dutch, late 17th century
38.7cm (15¼in)

[19] Ill. pl.65B in Charles Oman, *Caroline
Silver,* London, 1970

The Baroque idea developed differently in the several countries of Europe. In Italy the Baroque style, first manifest in the early seventeenth century, was an exuberant outburst of the Catholic Church's renewed spiritual authority and its recovery from the disruption caused by the Reformation. In northern Europe, particularly in France, the Baroque style had more of a secular than sacred significance: it was used to underline monarchical absolutism. The same was true, to a somewhat lesser extent, in England, where it was used to assure the position and power of a group of Whig noblemen rather than the monarchy. The architecture and appurtenances of royal and aristocratic houses became increasingly imbued with a classical stateliness to inspire this effect.

One of the simplest and most practical ways to light a room was with one or more wall-lights. In the seventeenth century these were often very elaborate affairs, used to show the status of the owner.

94

95

96

97

The three sets of silver wall-sconces (nos 98–100) each have a different method of depicting ownership on the backplate: chased, cast and engraved. Engraving is the most commonly found, or, as in the case of the brass example of no.97, the cartouche can be left vacant and thus simply acts as a reflector.

98 A silver wall-sconce (from a set of ten)
English
Four backplates: I.N. above a bird, London, 1668; the remainder: Robert Smythier; the branches: *c*1690, Arthur Manwaring
36.8cm (14½in)
These sconces are rather late examples of the auricular style. They are chased with the cypher of Charles II, whose illegitimate son, the Duke of Monmouth, married Anne, Countess of Buccleuch.
    Smythier's mark also appears on six sconces in the collection of H.M. The Queen,[20] and, collaborating with the same maker, on a set of four dated 1668.[21] See also no.88.

(The Duke of Buccleuch and Queensberry, KT)

99 A silver wall-sconce (from a set of six)
London, 1687
Thomas Jenkins[22]
31.7cm (12½in)

100 A silver wall-sconce
English, *c*1675
45cm (17¼in)
This sconce, from a set of four, is unmarked. This was quite common at this time in England, usually for pieces made on commission.
    Applied with the pierced monogram E.A.E below an earl's coronet for Anne, Countess of Exeter; she married in 1670 John, who succeeded as 5th Earl in 1678.

(The Burghley House collection)

101 A miniature collage of an interior
Italian, *c*1690
46cm (18in) high
With mirror-backed wall-lights (branches now lacking), which shows that they were hung above head height.

98

99

100

101

[20] Ill. pl.63B in Charles Oman, *Caroline Silver*, London, 1970

[21] Ill. pl.64A in Charles Oman, *Caroline Silver*, London, 1970

[22] For information on the work of this maker see A. Grimwade and J. Banister, 'Thomas Jenkins Unveiled', *Connoisseur*, August, 1974. His work is always of high quality and, in designs such as tankards, closely associated with that of Jacob Bodendick and the maker I.H. (see no.88)

102

102 A silver wall-light
London, 1701; the unmarked
sconce probably later
Thomas Corbett
27cm (10½in)

103 Three silver wall-sconces
(from a set of six)
London, 1730
Peter Archambo
41cm (16in)
The centres chased with
mythological scenes: Diana and
Actaeon, Prometheus bound,
Perseus and Andromeda,
Tantalus with Ixion and Sisyphus
in the distance, the death of
Phaethon and Narcissus and
Echo.
  These sconces were made fifty
years later than those of nos
98–100, but are obviously
inspired by the 17th-century
examples. They were made for
George Booth, 2nd Earl of
Warrington (1675–1758) and
engraved with his monogram and

coronet. George Booth was an
important patron of Huguenot
goldsmiths, placing orders with
makers such as Isaac Liger, James
Shruder and David Willaume II;
however Peter Archambo was
responsible for most of his
commissions until about 1728.
The majority of Booth's plate was
made in the very plain style
popular in England in the early
18th century; the Earl remained
loyal to this taste well after it went
out of fashion. These sconces are
unusual in his collection for their
elaborate design.[23]

104 A silver wall-sconce
London, 1699
John Bache
30cm (11¾in)
This is an unusually elaborate
form of this type of sconce;
similar examples are also found
on the Continent.[24]

*(The Governor and Company of the
Bank of England)*

103

104

[23] For further information on George Booth and his collection
see the sale catalogue entry for the sconces in this book

[24] For example a pair made in Avignon, with elegantly cut
holes to remove the spent candles, ill. in Claude Gérard
Cassan, 'Les Orfèvres d'Avignon', *Art & Curiosité*,
April–June 1984 edn., p.60

At the end of the seventeenth and beginning of the eighteenth century there emerged a taste for very plain silver, particularly in England. The style was then copied by base-metal workers (nos 106–115, 176). It was contemporary with the sophisticated French style (nos 124, 138 & 146), based on the designs of Jean Bérain, Daniel Marot, de Moelder and others, which were circulated in printed pattern books and widely used by all craftsmen, and which reached the height of popularity in the 1720s (see nos 105, 118 & 132). In both the plain (sometimes known as 'Queen Anne') and the decorated ('Régence') style, the craftsmen developed shapes for the baluster candlestick peculiar to their country.

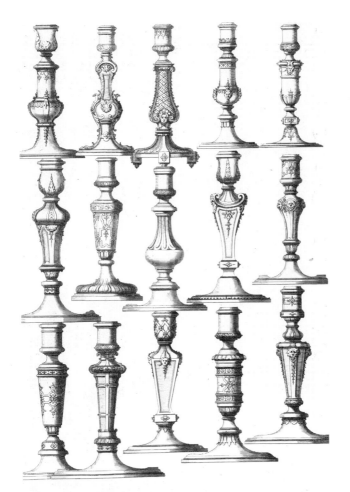

105

106

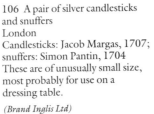

106 A pair of silver candlesticks and snuffers
London
Candlesticks: Jacob Margas, 1707; snuffers: Simon Pantin, 1704
These are of unusually small size, most probably for use on a dressing table.

(Brand Inglis Ltd)

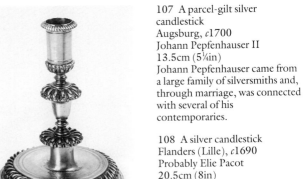

107

107 A parcel-gilt silver candlestick
Augsburg, *c*1700
Johann Pepfenhauser II
13.5cm (5¼in)
Johann Pepfenhauser came from a large family of silversmiths and, through marriage, was connected with several of his contemporaries.

108 A silver candlestick
Flanders (Lille), *c*1690
Probably Elie Pacot
20.5cm (8in)

109 A bronze candlestick
Probably French, *c*1690

(Peter Hempson)

108

109

110

110 A silver candlestick
Spanish, *c*1700

(Brand Inglis Ltd)

111 A silver candlestick
London, 1702
William Denny
16.5cm (6½in)

112 A silver candlestick
London, 1710
David Willaume I
15.2cm (6in)
Engraved with the Royal arms.
   David Willaume (1658–1741)
was one of the finest silversmiths
of the early 18th century. A
Huguenot from Metz, he is
recorded as being in London
from 1686. He married the sister
of Lewis Mettayer and their
daughter married David
Tanqueray. Unlike so many of his
contemporaries who went
bankrupt, he was a successful
businessman, with a large and
wealthy clientele.

113 A silver candlestick
London, 1719
Isaac Liger
7in (18.2cm)
One of a pair engraved with
scratch weights: 16 and 15 = 16.
When sold in 1990 the weight of
these candlesticks was 30oz.7dwt,
showing that they have lost
1oz.9dwt through wear and
cleaning. As silver in the 18th
century was sold by its weight,
with a charge for fashioning per
ounce, it was a common practice
to engrave the weight on the
underside of the object.

111

112

113

114 A pair of silver candlesticks
Dutch (Nijmegen), 1710
Bernt Wolff
21cm (8¼in)

115 A pewter candlestick
English (Newcastle), *c*1720
George Lowes
16.5cm (96½in)
English pewter candlesticks of the early 18th
century are rare, the market having been taken
over by brass.

(Peter Hornsby)

114

115

This tiny den with the unusual luxury of a fireplace was on the half-landing of Saint-Simon's first small apartment at Versailles. When the door was closed it was pitch dark. It held a table, two chairs and a cupboard. It was comfortable; better, it was private. Two men could talk there unheard, their faces almost touching across the table between two lighted candles.

Historical Memoirs of the Duc de Saint-Simon, 1691–1723; note by the editor, Lucy Norton, London, 1972

. . . and then Commissioner Pett (who was by at all my discourse, and this held till within an hour after candle-light, for I had candles brought in to read my papers by) was to answer for himself . . .

Diary of Samuel Pepys, 22 September 1667

The Servants' candlesticks are generally broken, for nothing lasts forever. But you may find out expedients; you may conveniently stick your candle in a bottle . . . or upon its own grease upon a table . . . or you may cut a hole in a loaf and stick it in there.

JONATHAN SWIFT, *Directions to Servants,* 1745

Avoid burning daylight, and to save your master's candles never bring them up till half an hour after it be dark, although they are called for ever so often.

. . . There is nothing wherein the skill of a butler more appears than in the management of candles.

JONATHAN SWIFT, *Directions to Servants,* 1745

A horrid hole of a house, in an alley they call a court; stairs wretchedly narrow, even to the first floor rooms: and into a den they led me, with broken walls which had been papered, as I saw by a multitude of tacks, and some torn bits held on by the rusty heads.

The floor indeed was clean, but the ceiling was smoked with a variety of figures. . . . An old, tottering, wormeaten table, that had more nails bestowed in mending it to make it stand, than the table cost fifty years ago when new.

On the mantelpiece was an iron shove-up candlestick, with a lighted candle in it, twinkle, twinkle, twinkle, four of them, I suppose, for a penny.

SAMUEL RICHARDSON, *Clarissa,* 1747

117 A boy blowing on a firebrand to light a candle
Godfried Schalcken
(1643–1706)
This painting was probably executed in the mid-1690s and shows a brass long-handled candlestick typical of this period, though in a style that was continued well into the 18th century.

Schalcken moved to England in 1692, remaining there for five years, during which time he painted at least five canvases for Robert Spencer, 2nd Earl of Sunderland (1641–1702), including the present picture. The painting was famous in the 18th century, at which time it was copied and engraved, possibly because of the disguised allusion to the lusty youth lighting the flame of passion, a type of symbolism well understood by contemporary connoisseurs.

(Artemis Fine Art)
(Now in the National Galleries of Scotland, Edinburgh, recently acquired with help from the National Art-Collections Fund)

116 A silver chamber candlestick
London, 1700
12cm (4¾in) diam

116

117

The development of the wall-sconce from the embossed or cast oval backplate to the more architectural form shown in nos 123–124, can be seen in the designs of Daniel Marot. Whereas the late seventeenth-century silver wall-sconces (as seen in nos 98–100) have survived in quite large sets in some English country houses, the early eighteenth-century form shown here is rarer. The wall-light became ever more popular and in the first half of the eighteenth century examples are to be found in brass, iron, gilded bronze and wood, as well as in silver.

118

119

118 Designs for candle-holders, sconces etc
C. de Moelder

(Trustees of the Victoria & Albert Museum, London)

119 A gilded bronze wall-light
French, early 18th century
30cm (11¾in)

120

120 Design for a candle-branch for a chandelier or wall-sconce
German school, probably *c*1700

(Houthakker collection)

121 An iron pricket wall-sconce
Austrian, 1st half 18th century
56cm (22in) long

121

122 A gilt-brass wall-lantern
English, *c*1725
74cm (29in)

123 A gilded bronze wall-light
French, *c*1715
33cm (13in)

124 A silver-gilt wall-sconce
London, *c*1713–15
Paul de Lamerie
56cm (22in)
Engraved with the arms of Thomas Foley,
created Baron Foley of Kidderminster in
1712; he died in 1733.

Until the exhibition of Paul de Lamerie's
work in 1990,[25] this pair of sconces (only one
is illustrated) had been dated *c*1720–25,
however after close examination of the
maker's mark, they are now given an earlier
date. They are made in Britannia Standard, the
higher standard of silver that was compulsory
in England between 1697 and 1720. Unlike
most of his contemporaries, who then
reverted to using Sterling standard silver,
Lamerie continued to work only in Britannia
Standard until 1732.

These sconces are among the finest of
Lamerie's early work, showing full
understanding of the designs of Daniel Marot
in his use of a narrow cast backplate with
double branches. As can be seen in
contemporary engravings, such sconces were
placed on either side of a fireplace or looking-
glass.

(Now in the Gilbert collection, Los Angeles)[26]

122

123

124

[25] *Paul de Lamerie*, exh. cat., ed. Susan Hare, Goldsmiths'
Hall, London, 1990, no.8

[26] Timothy B. Schroder, *The Gilbert Collection of Gold and
Silver*, Los Angeles, 1988, no.39

125

126

125 The Galerie d'Hercule at the hôtel Lambert, Paris
3rd quarter 17th century
After designs by Louis Le Vau (1612–70)
The gallery has reliefs by Le Sueur and a painted ceiling by Le Brun showing scenes of Hercules' life and labours. The furniture is ranged along the walls and interspaced with gilded wood torchères supporting candelabra of what is known as 'girandole' form in France. It is unlikely that the room ever had hanging chandeliers and the sombre colours and subdued candle-light still make it wonderfully mysterious at night. This must be more or less the way it was always lit.

The term girandole is confusing as in England it has referred, certainly since the 18th century, to a form of wall-light with mirrored backplate and candle-branches. It was originally named after a kind of Italian firework, a *girandola*, that revolved like a horizontal Catherine wheel.

A torchère, or torchier, originally supported one thick candle made of several rods of wax twisted (*torsé*) together, but the term came to be used for any stand which supported a candelabrum, and later the candle-branches were sometimes attached to the stand (see no.320)

126 A gilded bronze and boulle torchère
French, *c*1700
Attributed to André-Charles Boulle
141cm (4ft 7½in)
Though possibly originally intended to support some form of sculpture, a bust perhaps, this pedestal was more likely part of a larger set which was ranged around a big formal room to support candelabra. It is taken directly from a design by André-Charles Boulle. A set of six is in the Louvre in Paris, stamped by the late 18th-century ébéniste Etienne Levasseur, who doubtless repaired them at some time and was obliged by guild laws to stamp them. Other pairs also exist and all have the unusual fringed apron hanging below the frieze. These have a translucent shell background, from the underbelly of the turtle, which has been painted blue on the reverse.

This torchère is one of a pair which belonged to Lord Carnarvon at Highclere Castle and was probably formerly in the Alfred de Rothschild collection, inherited by his illegitimate daughter, who married the Earl of Carnarvon.

127 A pair of gilded and patinated bronze candlesticks
French, early 18th century

128 A gilded bronze candlestick
French, *c*1700
In the manner of Claude Ballin

127

128

129

130

131 A pair of gilded bronze candlesticks
French, early 18th century
Perhaps cast by the goldsmith Claude Ballin
39.5cm (15½in)
A pair of candlesticks whose description exactly fits the present examples was in the sale of the deceased Marquis de Marigny's possessions in March 1782 under lot 376: 'Une autre paire (de flambeaux), dont le corps est en bronze et représente, l'un une femme montée sur un dauphin, l'autre un satyre et un tigre. Les pieds et les bobèches sont en cuivre doré.' This pair of candlesticks, along with another pair showing a man and a woman carrying children, the previous lot in the Marigny sale, were almost certainly cast by the goldsmith Ballin. They were in the sale of M. de Selle in 1761 (lots 154 and 155) and the catalogue of that sale mentions: 'Feu M. de Selle les a acquis à la vente du Sieur Ballin, Orfèvre du Roi'.[27]

Gabriel Huquier (1695–1772)[28] engraved designs after Gilles-Marie Oppenord (1672–1742), *Quatrième Livre Contenant des Montans ou Pilastres*, including a female figure apparently derived from a 16th-century etching which could have provided the inspiration for the sea nymph stem in one of the present candlesticks.

Abel-François de Vandières (1727–81), Marquis de Marigny and de Menars, brother of Madame de Pompadour, was created 'directeur général des bâtiments, jardins, arts, académies et manufactures royales' in 1751, at the age of twenty-four, having previously been sent to study in Italy.

Claude Ballin (1661–1754) was received as Master in 1688. His uncle, also Claude Ballin (1615–78), was Master in 1637 and 'orfèvre du Roi' by 1646; he was responsible for much of the silver made for Louis XIV at Versailles but his work is known to us today through his designs.

129 A pair of gold candlesticks
Brussels, c1755
Petrus Josephus Fonson
34.8cm (13¾in)
Made for Charles de Lorrain (d.1780), brother of Emperor Francis I. The candlesticks are part of a service, which includes a table centre-piece with four candle-holders, in the Rococo style, of gold, gilded brass and porcelain.[28]

(Kunsthistorisches Museum, Vienna)

130 A gilded bronze candlestick
French, mid-19th century
33.7cm (13¼in)
The design is based on a Louis XIV model (no.128)

131

[27] A. Pradère, 'L'Ameublement de Marigny', *L'Estampille*, May/July 1986

[28] Ill. p.126 in M.Leithe-Jasper and R. Distelberger, *The Kunsthistorisches Museum Vienna*, London, 1982

132 Design for centrepieces and candelabra
French, early 18th century
Jean Bérain

(Trustees of the Victoria & Albert Museum, London)

133 A silver centrepiece
London, 1731
David Willaume II and Anne Tanqueray
56cm (22in) overall
Engraved with the arms of Cholmley Turner
of Kirkleatham, Member of Parliament for
York.

The centrepiece containing alternative
settings first appeared in the late 17th century
in France. Whilst an impressive and expensive
idea, they were short-lived, giving way in the
mid-18th century to the epergne (see
no.325), which contained dishes for fruit and
sweetmeats, and sometimes candle-holders,
but did not incorporate a tureen, casters and
cruets as does this example. Accounts describe
the early 18th-century form as a 'machine' or
'surtout compleat'. The amount of light given
by this centrepiece would have been adequate
for an intimate table, but the lighted candles
must have made it awkward to reach the food.

Similar centrepieces were made, for
example, by Paul de Lamerie in 1734 (now in
Moscow) and 1736[29] and, in the Rococo
taste, by Augustin Courtauld in 1741.[30] James
Lomax has estimated that this centrepiece
might have cost about £340.[31]

(Now in Temple Newsam House, Leeds)

[29] *Paul de Lamerie*, exh. cat., ed. Susan Hare, Goldsmiths'
Hall, London, 1990, nos 40 and 87

[30] Now in the Hermitage, Leningrad, ill. in *Ori e argenti
dall'Ermitage*, exh. cat., Lugano, 1986, no.6

[31] James Lomax, 'A Silver Centrepiece for Temple Newsam',
National Art-Collections Fund Review, 1989

132

133a

133b

134

135

134 Design for a centrepiece
German, early 18th century
From a set of designs by Joh:
Leonhard Wüst, engraved by
Jeremias Wolff

(Private collection)

135 A gilded bronze and
porcelain candelabrum
early 18th century
The porcelain: Chinese, *c*1700;
the mounts: French
38cm (15in)
The nozzles, drip-pans, stem and
base of this candelabrum are
made of Chinese blanc-de-chine
domestic objects – tea-bowls,
saucers and the base of a bowl.
The finial and feet are made of
blanc-de-chine figures riding
Kylins.

A candlestick with branches
was known as a *candelabre* in
France, literally a tree of candles,
and was translated to
candelabrum in English.

136 A brass table centrepiece
French, early 18th century
As was the case with many early
18th-century candlesticks which
are now brass, this piece was
originally silver-plated. Traces of
silver remain though most has
worn away.

(Brian Beet)

137 A gilded bronze table
centrepiece
French, early 18th century
40cm (15½in)
A covered tureen, with four
detachable candle branches.

136

137

138

139

140

138 A silver candlestick
Paris, 1729
Jacques Besnier
23.5cm (9¼in)
The design, possibly derived from
Jean Bérain, is similar to
candlesticks made in France from
the 1690s, in the Régence taste.

*(The Metropolitan Museum of Art,
New York, bequest of Catherine
D.Wentworth)*

139 A silver candlestick
Flemish (Liège), 1717
Charles de Hontoir
20.3cm (8in)

140 A silver candlestick
Cologne, c1700
Probably Johannes Speltz
23cm (9in)

141 Four silver candlesticks
London
Anthony Nelme, 1691; and
Joseph Bird, 1702
13.3cm and 17.2cm (5¼in and
6¾in)

142 A toilet candlestick
Paris, 1714-15
Gilles Gouel
12cm (4¾in)

141

143 An agate and silver-gilt
candlestick
German, c1720–25
15.9cm (6¼in)
Although the mounts are
unmarked, these candlesticks
were probably made in Augsburg,
possibly in the workshop of
Tobias Baur, who specialized in
the mounting of hardstones and
enamel, particularly for toilet sets.

(Timothy Schroder Ltd)

142

143

144

144 A pair of silver candlesticks
Groningen, 1723
Johannes van der Lely
Johannes van der Lely was made a
master in 1695, and was the
foremost silversmith in Friesland
at this period, specializing in
embossed decoration.

(H.S. Wellby Ltd)

145 A pair of silver candlesticks
London, 1727
Paul Crespin
21.8cm (8½in)
This design of candlestick, in the
French Régence taste, was made
by other makers also, for example
David Willaume in 1730.[32] It is
very close to Parisian examples.
These candlesticks, engraved with
the arms of George II, are one of
eleven pairs issued from the Royal
Jewel House to Philip Stanhope,
4th Earl of Chesterfield, as part of
his official plate on his
appointment as Ambassador to
The Hague in 1728, where he

remained until 1732. Among his
other plate was a pair of wine
coolers bearing the mark of Paul
de Lamerie overstruck by that of
Paul Crespin.[33]

Lord Chesterfield was
responsible for the passing of the
Act in 1751 which altered the
reckoning of the calendar from
the Julian to the Gregorian style.
However, he is chiefly famous for
his letters to his illegitimate son,
Philip Stanhope.[34]

[32] Sotheby's, London, 5 February 1987,
lot 98

[33] Sold at Sotheby's, London, 4 February
1988, lot 112, now in the Victoria &
Albert Museum, London and the National Museum
of Scotland, Edinburgh

[34] First published in 1774

145

146

147

146 A gilded bronze candlestick
French, c1720
23cm (9in)

147 A colour-twist glass
candlestick
English
20.5cm (8in)
With central opaque-gauze core
entwined with opaque-white and
translucent royal-blue threads

148

149

148 A glass candlestick, with oil
lamp
Liège, c1690–1700
The oil lamp attachment, possibly
of slightly later date than the
candlestick, provides a double use
for this object.

(Brand Inglis Ltd)

149 A glass candlestick
English, c1710
18.5cm (7¼in)

The French word chandelier originally signified a holder for tallow candles (*chandelles*) as opposed to wax candles (*bougies*). By the seventeenth century the term had come to mean a holder for any sort of candles though not specifically suspended from the ceiling as it has now come to mean in England. Chandeliers hung with drops of glass or rock-crystal were known as *lustres* in France, and this has become the generic term for all hanging chandeliers.

150

150 A banquet at the palace of the cardinal of Regensburg, 1717

(Trustees of the Science Museum, London)

151 Drawing of a chandelier Gaetano Guadro, *c*1730 Amber, silver and rock-crystal

(Trustees of the Victoria & Albert Museum, London)

151

195

196

195 A porcelain candlestick
Meissen, *c*1740
After a design by Meissonnier
24cm (9½in)
Incised 46, originally modelled
by Eberlein for the Swan service,
which was made for Count Brühl,
the aristocratic over-seer of the
Meissen factory. The service was
ordered in 1739, though it took
several years to make.

The service disappeared and
was only discovered after World
War II in a pond, where it had
possibly been hidden having been
stolen by gypsies.

196 A pair of gilded bronze
candlesticks
French, *c*1745
After a design by Meissonnier
32.5cm (12¾in)
Each candlestick is struck with a
small crowned C mark, which was
a tax mark used from 1745–49
on any alloy utilizing copper.

197

197 A pair of Delft candlesticks
Dutch (the Young Moor's Head
factory), *c*1760
J.V.D.H. mark
21.5cm (8½in)
Jan van der Hagen was proprietor
of the factory 1732–64.

198 A pair of porcelain
candlesticks
Meissen, mid-18th century
23.8cm (9¼in)

198

199

200

201

202

203

199 A pair of silver candlesticks
London, 1734
Lewis Pantin
29cm (11½in); 2,500gr
(80oz.10dwt)
Engraved with the crest of Sir
Watkin Williams-Wynn.

1734 is early for such
sophisticated examples of the
Rococo in England.

200 A pair of silver candlesticks
London, 1745
Lewis Pantin
31cm (12¼in); 3,016gr (97oz)
The twisted column stem is
seldom found in silver
candlesticks. Other English
makers to have used it are Peter
Archambo,[41] and Herne & Butty,
in 1760.[42]

(Christie's)

201 A silver candlestick
London, 1746
Nicholas Sprimont
26.8cm (10½in); 1,878gr (60oz
8dwt) scratch weight 62 0 oz
Nicholas Sprimont, from Liège,
registered his mark in London in
January 1742. By September
1744 he was producing porcelain
in Chelsea and stopped working
as a silversmith some time after
Christmas 1748.

He appears to have been closely
connected with Paul Crespin, but
the exact nature of their
involvement is not yet known,
just as Crespin's involvement with
Lamerie is still unclear.[43] An
identical pair of candlesticks to
this, bearing the mark of Paul de
Lamerie, is dated 1747 [44] The
most famous piece on which
Sprimont and Crespin are
thought to have collaborated is
the centrepiece of 1741 in the
collection of H.M. The Queen,
possibly ordered through George
Wickes for Frederick, Prince of
Wales.[45]

202 A pair of silver candlesticks
London, 1751
Alexander Johnston
27cm (10½in);1,430gr (46oz)

(Christie's)

203 A pair of silver candlesticks
London, 1743
Frederick Kandler
29.2cm (11½in); 2,094gr (67oz
7dwt)

The candlesticks shown in nos 199–203 are all out of the ordinary, by leading London makers in the 1730s and 1740s. Neither Pantin, Sprimont nor Kandler were of English origin and Alexander Johnston's candlesticks are closer to French models than English. The quality of their design and manufacture is very different to those made for stock or for more general sale, such as those illustrated in nos 174 and 265. Their weight and size gives an indication of original cost and quality – an 'average' pair of mid-18th-century English candlesticks, between 6½in and 9in (16.5cm and 23cm) high, weighs between 25oz and 45oz (777gr and 1,400 gr).

The same distinction between 'good' and 'average' quality pieces can, of course, be found throughout Europe – for example in the German candlesticks from Dresden (no.224) and Augsburg (no.217).

[41] Ill. in Judith Banister, 'Peter Archambo, Master of elegant silver', Country Life, 9 June 1983

[42] Sotheby's, London, 1 March 1962, lot 143

[43] See wine coolers, Sotheby's, 4 February 1988, lot 112

[44] The Glory of the Goldsmith, exh. cat., Christie's, London, 1989, no.96

[45] Treasures from the Royal Collection, exh. cat., Buckingham Palace, London, 1988, no.114

204 A silver candlestick from
four matching, dated
Paris, 1749, 1753 and 1761
Louis-Joseph Lenhendrick
27cm (10½in)
The design of this model has been
attributed to Thomas Germain,
to whom Lenhendrick was
apprenticed.[46] Its popularity can
be seen in the span of years over
which these four matching
candlesticks were made.
Lenhendrick was a fine
silversmith, who collaborated
with F-T. Germain and R-J.
Auguste in major commissions,
for example the Orloff service for
Catherine the Great of Russia (see
no.393).

205 A silver candlestick
London, 1741
Paul de Lamerie
22.3cm (8¾in)

206 A silver candlestick
Paris, 1735
26cm (10¼in)
When sold in 1956, the maker's
mark was described as P.F.B.,
initials which do not exactly
match those of two likely
candidates for the production of
candlesticks of this quality:
Besnier or Balzac.

207 A silver candlestick, with
later branches for two lights and
five lights (illustrated)
London
Candlestick: Paul de Lamerie,
1731; branches: Ebenezer Coker,
1774
Candlestick: 24.1cm (9½in); five-
light candelabrum: 38.7cm
(15¼in)
This design of candlestick proved
to be one of Lamerie's most
popular models. The example
illustrated here has later branches:
both the two-light and five-light
versions are very different to
those made by Lamerie for
identical candlesticks in the same
year[47] for four lights. A pair of
three-light candelabra of 1736
has the same stems but more
elaborate bases.[48] That in no.205,
whilst obviously based on the
same design, in fact varies in
almost every detail.
  The practice of adding
branches at a later date was quite
common, either to replace
damaged branches or to alter the
use. Perhaps the most frequently
found alterations are those made

by early 19th-century makers,
such as Rundell, Bridge &
Rundell or Robert Garrard, to
18th-century pieces. The four
candlesticks after designs by
William Kent, for example
(no.225) have branches bearing
the mark of Paul Storr (not
illustrated), whilst the chandelier
of no.153 has additional branches
by Hunt & Roskell.

208 A silver candlestick
Paris, 1755
Jacques-Nicolas Roettiers
28cm (11in)

209 A silver candlestick
London, 1737
George Wickes
25.4cm (10in)
George Wickes (1698–1761)
registered his first mark in 1721
and was goldsmith to Frederick
Prince of Wales from 1735. One
of the foremost silversmiths of the
mid-18th century in London, his
firm continued under the
partnership of Parker and Wakelin
(see no.222)
  As in the case of nos 205 and
207, this design was made by
Wickes over a number of years,[49]
with variations in detail. Elaine
Barr[50] illustrates four unmarked
examples. It is interesting that
two important makers, Lamerie
and Wickes, should produce
designs in many respects so
similar.

*(The Worshipful Company of
Goldsmiths, London)*

[46] Faith Denis, *Three Centuries of French Domestic Silver*, New York, 1960, no.224

[47] In the Gilbert collection, Los Angeles, cat. no.50; see also *Paul de Lamerie*, exh. cat, ed. Susan Hare, Goldsmiths' Hall, London, 1990, no.52, with the crest of Sir Robert Walpole

[48] Al Tajir collection, *The Glory of the Goldsmith*, exh. cat., Christie's, London, 1989, no.73

[49] For example a pair of 1742, Christie's, Geneva, 14 November 1972

[50] Elaine Barr, *George Wickes*, London, 1980, fig.65b

204

205

206

207

208

209

210 A silver chamber candlestick
French (Nîmes), 1752
Louis Mastre I
19.7cm (7¾in) long

211 A porcelain chamber
candlestick, painted in underglaze
blue
English (Worcester), c1768-70

(Simon Spero)

212 A silver chamber candlestick
German (Naumberg), c1750
Maker's mark C.G.B.
12.5cm (5in) diam

213 A silver chamber candlestick
Rome, c1775
Luigi Valadier

214 A silver chamber candlestick
London, 1744
Paul Crespin
17.8cm (7in) wide
This design was copied in the
19th century by C.T. & G. Fox.[51]

215 A porcelain chamber
candlestick
Hochst, c1765–70
7.5cm (3in)

210

211

212

213

214

215

[51] For an example, London 1842, see
Sotheby's Belgravia, London, 13 April 1978,
lot 171

216   217   218   219

220

216 A silver candelabrum
Brussels, 1752

(H.S. Wellby Ltd)

217 A silver candelabrum
Augsburg, 1761–63
J.P.Heckenauer
47.6cm (18¾in)
From the collection of Friedrich Wilhelm,
Freiherr von Westphalen zu Furstenberg
(1727–89), Prince-Bishop of Hildesheim,
near Hanover in Germany, from 7 February
1763.

218 A silver candlestick
Lausanne, c1785
Walter Brenner
22.7cm (9in)

219 A silver candlestick
New York, c1760–70
Daniel Christian Fueter
21.3cm (8½in)
Much of the silver and pewter made in
America in the 18th century is based on
designs common in the homeland of the
maker. Fueter (1720–85) came from Berne in
Switzerland and comparison of this
candlestick with the one illustrated as no.218
shows how closely he followed a fashionable
Swiss style.

220 Eight silver candlesticks
Augsburg, 1765–67 and
1773–75

221 Four silver candlesticks
Amsterdam, 1765
Casper Valentijn Beumke
25cm (9¾in)

222 A pair of silver candlesticks
London, 1755
Edward Wakelin
Edward Wakelin joined George
Wickes in 1747 and on the latter's
retirement in 1760 took over his
firm in partnership with John
Parker. The firm of Parker and
Wakelin are the best chronicled
firm of 18th-century London
goldsmiths due to the fortunate
survival of many of their ledgers.[52]
John Römer, whose mark appears
on the candlestick of no.223, was
a senior workman in the firm,
possibly the works manager, and
probably related to the
Norwegian-born Emick Römer.

(Brand Inglis Ltd)

221   222   223

223 A silver candlestick
London, 1763
John Römer
25.5cm (10in)
In comparing objects it is
interesting to see how a workshop
develops a design over a period of
eight years. This candlestick is a
much simplified version of
no.222.

[52] Elaine Barr, *George Wickes*, London, 1980;
Dr Helen Clifford, 'The Organisation of an
Eighteenth Century Goldsmith's Business',
International Silver and Jewellery Fair,
London, 1990; Royal Goldsmiths, The
Garrard Heritage, exh.cat. 1991

224

224 Six silver candlesticks
Dresden, *c*1750
Christian Heinrich Ingermann
24.5cm (9½in)
Numbered 29–34 and engraved
with the cypher of Augustus III
(1733–63), Duke of Saxony and
King of Poland. A pair of identical
silver-gilt candlesticks by C.D.
Schroder, also engraved with the
cypher of Frederick Augustus,
were probably part of a set of
thirty-six.

225 Four silver-gilt candlesticks
London; Edward Wakelin, 1757
and John Parker & Edward
Wakelin, 1775; after designs by
William Kent. 30.7cm (12in)
high
The firm of George Wickes, later
Parker & Wakelin, made several
pieces after the designs of William
Kent (which were published by
John Vardy in 1744); notably a
gold cup, 1736, a mug, 1745, a
pair of tureens, 1744.

When these candlesticks were
sold in 1921[53] they were with four
others, by Paul Crespin, 1745,[54]
which are assumed to be of the
same design and the models for
the Wakelin examples. The 1757
pair was ordered by the 9th Earl of
Lincoln at a cost of £64.1s. He
became 2nd Duke of Newcastle in
1768 and paid £66.15s 7d for the
second pair (described as 'after
Kent' in the Wakelin ledgers) in
1775. Interestingly the charge for
fashioning went down from
14s.6d. per ounce for the first pair
(88oz 8dwt) to 14s. per ounce for
the second (95oz 8dwt).[55] Four
similar candlesticks, sold to the
Earl of Coventry in1758, weighed
188oz, 10dwt and cost £138 4s 8d
(now in the Al Tajir collection).

[53] Sale of plate from the Duke of Newcastle's
seat, Clumber, Worksop, Christie's, London,
7 July 1921, lots 53 and 54

[54] Four other candlesticks of a different
design survive by Crespin after Kent, dated
1741 (ill. in A.Grimwade, *Rococo Silver,*
London, 1974, pl.72A)

[55] Elaine Barr, *George Wickes,* London, 1980,
pp.101–3

225

226 A bronze lantern
French, c1725
110cm (43½in)

227 A gilded and black-japanned wood and glass wall-lantern
English, c1755
Made by the workshops of Jean Cuenot after designs by Giovanni Battista Borra for the staircase of Norfolk House, London
152cm (60in)

Norfolk House was built between 1748 and 1752 as a palatial London residence for the 9th Duke of Norfolk, to the designs of William Kent's former assistant Matthew Brettingham. It was demolished in 1938, but the Music Room interior survives.[56] Brettingham's façades were in an orthodox but uninspiring Palladian manner, but for the interior decoration the Duke turned to Giovanni Battista Borra, a Piedmontese architect.

Borra (1712–86) was a pupil of Vitone who worked extensively in Piedmont in the middle of the 18th century. Between 1740 and 1767 he collaborated with Alfieri on the Palazzo dell'Accademia Filarmonica in Turin, completing it after the death of the latter. He also worked for the Savoyard Prince, Ludovico Vittorio di Carignano, at the Palazzo Carignano in Turin and at the hunting lodge of Racconigi, just south of the Piedmontese capital. In 1750–51 he accompanied Robert Wood and James Dawkins on their expedition to Syria and Asia Minor and later prepared the drawings for the engraved plates of their two volumes *The Ruins of Palmyra* (1753) and *The Ruins of Baalbec* (1757). His documented commissions in England in the 1750s consist largely of work for Lord Temple in both the park and state apartments at Stowe, although his name has also been associated, on stylistic grounds, with work at Stratfield Saye and Woburn.

The Norfolk House lanterns were designed to hang over the door-cases in the staircase hall. A letter by William Farrington, dated 18 February 1756, describes a visit to Norfolk House and alludes to the lanterns '. . . then to the Stairs, wch are very large, & the Lights Beautifully Plac'd'.

The wood carving at Norfolk House was executed by John Antoine Cuenot, who employed both English and French craftsmen in his workshop. The lanterns are listed in the accounts as follows:

'To carving 2 illuminating lanthorns with an Eagle at the top of each, & a head in the middle   16. 12. 6d
To lining Do with tinn   3. 5. 0d'

They were delivered some time between 5 March 1753 and 24 February 1756. It seems likely that Cuenot was involved in other Borra commissions, including perhaps, the state bed from Stowe.[57]

Stylistically the lanterns are something of a mixture. The waisted cartouche shape is typical of Piedmontese Rococo while the Bérainesque masks and incised treillage add a Régence flavour, a feature of Borra's work. The rather Neo-classical anthemions, covering the smoke outlets, derive from motifs at Palmyra and were repeated in the frieze design around the ceiling, while the eagle crestings recall the work of William Kent.

[56] In the Victoria & Albert Museum, London

[57] Now in the Lady Lever Collection, Port Sunlight

226

227

228 Interior with card players
Pierre Louis Dumesnil the
younger (1698–1781)

*(The Metropolitan Museum of Art,
New York)*

229 Trade card of Anthony
Dyckhoff
Engraved by Gabriel Smith
'Tin-plate worker at the Lamp
and Crown the corner of Middle
Row Holbourn London
   Make Lamps for Halls,
Staircases and Chambers,
Likewise Tin Funnels for
Smoakey Chimneys, with all sorts
of Tin Wares in General. NB Fine
Spermaceti Oyl; & Lamps lighted
in the best Manner'
   The same trade card was used
by Dyckhoff's successor, David
Fontaine and the same design also
by Robert Thompson, whose
card is signed 'F.Garden Sculp
paternoster Row'.
   It was quite common for the
work of tin worker and
lamplighter to be carried out by
the same man. In 1801 Lucas &
Spencer, Tinplate workers & oil
men, charged £1.15s.6d. for
lighting two lamps from 18
January to 10 July.[58] Thirty years
earlier a Mr Turner received an
account from Evan Richards, Tin
man & Lamplighter to her Royal
Highness Princess Amelia 'To
Lighting a Lamp from 29
September 1769 to 24 June
1770, 9 months, £1.7.0.' which
he paid on 14 July 1770.[59]

*(Trustees of the British Museum,
London)*

230 Trade card of Ed Denby &
Wm Crook, Founders & Smiths
in Dean Street Soho

*(Trustees of the British Museum,
London)*

228

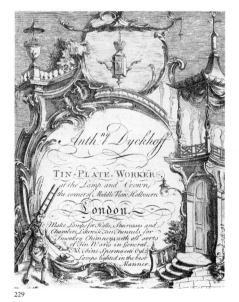

229

230

[58] Heal collection, British Museum, London

[59] Heal collection, British Museum, London

231 Le Souper fin
Jean-Michel Moreau le Jeune
(1741–1814)
This engraving is crammed with
items of interest for social
historians and students of the
decorative arts. Servants have
been banned from this intimate
supper, and there are small
serving tables by the guests. No
candles appear on the table, but a
lantern hangs above, lit by five
candles, and wall-lights give
further illumination.

*(Trustees of the Victoria & Albert
Museum, London)*

232 A gilded bronze lantern
French, mid-18th century
95.3cm (37½in)

232

231

233 Staircase, The Upper
Belvedere, Vienna (1720–21)
The architect J.L. von
Hildebrandt (1668–1745)
worked on the Belvedere for
Prince Eugene from 1714.
The metal lanterns would
originally have been lit with
candles.

234 A pair of gilded and painted
wood lanterns
Venetian, 1st half 18th century
231cm (7ft 7in)

235 A silver lantern, with purple-
wood shaft
Genoa, *c*1790
This was probably made for use in
a funeral procession. However,
once the ceremony had taken
place these very decorative
lanterns could be used in either a
domestic or church interior.

(Peter Hempson)

233

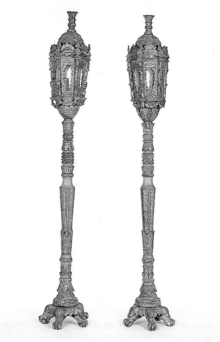

234

235

236 A gilded bronze wall-light
French, *c*1745
Struck with the crowned C mark (see note to
no.196)
71cm (28in)

237 A gilded bronze wall-light
Paris, dated 1756
François Thomas Germain
108cm (42½in)
This wall-light is signed: 'Fait par F.T. Germain
Sculp. Orf. du Roy Aux Galleries du Louvre à
Paris 1756'. On the back it is marked with the
crowned initials CP and No 28 and also '1051
Lux 2'. It is one from two pairs of wall-lights
originally made for the chambre d'apparat and
the salon des jeux of the duc d'Orléans at the
Palais Royal.

In 1756 the Palais Royal was redecorated to
the designs of the architect Contant d'Ivry, who
almost certainly would have designed the
furnishings as well as the architectural details. In
1762 Blondel described the work at the Palais
Royal as an ideal compromise between the
Rococo and classical – 'un juste milieu entre ces
deux excès'. In 1783 the wall-lights were sold to
the Crown and were, by 1786, in the salon des
nobles de la Reine at Compiègne – hence the
CP inventory mark. Under the Revolution they
were used to illuminate the residence of the
Directors at the Luxembourg Palace.

François-Thomas Germain, born in 1726,
became on the death of his father in 1748,
orfèvre and sculpteur du Roi, with lodgings at
the Louvre. Although his work as a silversmith is
justly famous, little is known of his activity as a
bronzier. Only two other works in gilded
bronze exist signed by him: a pair of chenets
made for Madame Infante,[60] and the mounts for
a chimney-piece made for the Count Bernstorff
in Copenhagen. There is some indication that
Germain provided items in gilded bronze for
Stanislas Poniatowski, King of Poland.

(Now in the J. Paul Getty Museum, Malibu)

238 A gilded bronze wall-light
French, mid-18th century
106cm (42in)

239 A gilded bronze wall-light
German or Austrian, *c*1730
43cm (17in)

236

237

238

239

[60] Now in the Louvre

240 Design for a girandole
English, mid-18th century
Matthias Lock

*(Trustees of the Victoria & Albert
Museum, London)*

241 A gilded wood and mirror-
glass girandole wall-light
English, mid-18th century
In the manner of Thomas
Johnson
107cm (42in)

242 A wrought-iron candle
holder
American, 18th century

*(The American Museum in Britain,
Bath)*

243 A gilded bronze hall lantern
English, *c*1770
64×122cm (25×48in)

*(Spencer House Ltd, photograph
Lucinda Lambton)*

242

240

241

243

The oil lamp had not advanced significantly in efficiency during the eighteenth century, whereas candles had become ever cleaner and brighter. Consequently the oil lamp seems to have fallen from favour at this time and very few examples dating from the first three quarters of the century seem to have survived or indeed appear to be depicted in contemporary paintings or engravings.

254

255a

255b

254 Design for a standing oil lamp
Workshop of Luigi Valadier (1726–85)
Luigi Valadier was the leading silversmith in Rome in the late 18th century. His father Andrea founded the firm, which on Luigi's death by suicide was continued by the latter's son, Giuseppe. The firm was run by Giuseppe Spagna from 1817 and closed c1880. See also nos. 1 and 213.[61]

(Trinity Fine Art Ltd)

255 Two interior scenes of families playing games
Giuseppe Piattoli (fl.1785–1807)

[61] *Valadier,* exh. cat., Artemis, London, 1991; and articles in *Apollo,* May 1991 on a collection of drawings from the workshop

256 A gilded wood torchère
French, early 1740s
After a design by François
Roumier for Versailles
192cm (6ft 3½in)
On 25 May 1743 the Slodtz
brothers and François Roumier
delivered twenty-eight guéridons
or torchères to Versailles of three
different designs, for use in the
Grands Appartements du Roi –
two sets of ten and a set of eight.
Roumier executed one of the sets
of ten:
  'Du 25 may 1743 Slodtz et
Roumier guéridon pour les
grands appartements de Versailles
  No. 1302 Roumier
Livré par les Srs Slodtz fréres et
Roumier, Sculpteurs, les
guéridons de bois sculpté. Pour
servir dans les grands
appartements du Roy au chateau
de Versailles.
  Dix guéridons de bois sculpté
doré de 6 pieds de haut, les
plateaux travaillés en forme de
rocailles au dessous desquels sont
des plantes, fleurs et fruits chinois
tournans autour de la tige.
Ensuite sont trois cartouches des
armes de france, entourés de
rocailles et aiant sur les angles, des
branches de chênes d'olives et de
laurier. Au milieu qui est a jour,
est un cul de lampe renversé,
terminé d'une graine, par le bas
sont trois cartouches ovales
chargés des chiffres du roy le pied
formé par trois consoles, en
dehors enrichi de feuilles,
cannelures et autres ornemens.'
  The guéridons by Roumier were
intended for use in the salon de
Mars which was Louis XV's ball-
room, the sets by the Slodtz
brothers for the chambre du
trône and the salon de Mercure.
The design on which the present
torchère is based is in the
Bibliothèque du Roi.[62]
  Sebastien Slodtz (1655–1726)
was a pupil of Girardon and a
grandson of the cabinet-maker
Domenico Cucci. Three of his
sons worked for the Crown both
as sculptors and designers –
Antoine Sebastien
(c1695–1754), Paul Amboise
(1702–58) a member of the
Academie Royale in 1743, and
Réné Michel (1705–64) – all
three were made Dessinateur de
la chambre du Roi in succession.

[62](B.N.Est., Hd64)

256

257

258

259

257 A carved, gilded and painted wood torchère
English, *c*1750
Attributed to Matthias Lock

258 A kingwood parquetry and gilded bronze corner cabinet
French, *c*1740
Stamped by the maker Jacques Dubois
325.5cm (9ft 6in)
Taken from a design by Nicolas Pineau[63] in a less full-bodied Rococo style. The design shows the four candle-branches with lighted candles.

(Now in the J.Paul Getty Museum, Malibu)

259 Design for a torchère
Signed on the reverse: M.May, 2 juin 1750
Michael May came from a family of goldsmiths working in Kronstadt and died in 1776. The design of this torchère harks back to French originals of some twenty-five years earlier.

(Houthakker collection)

[63] Now in the Musée des Arts Décoratifs, Paris

260

As the eighteenth century progressed, it became possible to furnish a home with a wider variety of materials. No longer was the alternative to silver restricted to base metals or earthenware. The increased prosperity of the middle classes was catered for in a broadening of the quality of objects available and thus in their cost. Nos 260–265 show how the various trades copied designs or followed stylistic trends – led by silversmiths. Brassworkers followed the work of silversmiths particularly closely and later in the century Sheffield Plate and Britannia Metal gave purchasers even more choice.

261

262

264

265

260 An opaque-white glass candlestick
English (Staffordshire), *c*1760
22.8cm (9in)

261 An enamel candlestick
English (Bilston), *c*1770
28cm (11in)

262 A brass candlestick
English, *c*1755
(*Peter Hempson*)

263 A pair of glass candlesticks
English, *c*1765
25.7cm (10in)
With opaque-twist composite stems.

264 A porcelain candlestick
English (Vauxhall), *c*1755–60
A rare survival of this type of candlestick in porcelain.

(*Simon Spero*)

263

265 A pair of silver candlesticks
London, 1751/2
John Cafe
22.3cm (8¾in)
William Cafe and his brother John were specialist candlestick-makers. Large quantities of their work have survived, suggesting that they probably supplied a high proportion of the trade with cast candlesticks in the middle of the 18th century.

Figural representations became increasingly popular during the eighteenth century as supports for candlesticks and candelabra. Many ingenious variations were designed, sometimes using the arms to support the nozzles, more often the head, and sometimes adding a tree behind from which the candle-branches seemed to grow almost naturally.

266 Two silver candlesticks
English, *c*1740–45
Unmarked, after a design by
George Michael Moser
37.5cm (14¾in)
From a set of four, depicting
Apollo and Daphne.[64]
   Moser (1706–83) is chiefly
renowned for his work as a
modeller, enameller and chaser,
particularly in gold. He was
born in Schaffhausen,
Switzerland and taught in
London at the St. Martins Lane
Academy (founded by William
Hogarth).
*(Now in the Victoria & Albert
Museum, London)*

267 A gilded bronze
candelabrum
English, early 19th century
Signed: Frisbee fecit
43in (17in)
William Frisbee is recorded
working with the silversmith Paul
Storr in Cock Lane, London, in
the early 1790s and died in 1820.
It is unusual that the gilded
bronze model appears to be more
finished than its silver counterpart
in no.268.

268 A silver candelabrum
London, 1742
James Shruder, the branches
unmarked
37.5cm (14¾in)

[64] See *Pattern and Design*, exh. cat., Victoria
& Albert Museum, London, 1983

266a

266b

267

268

269 A silver candelabrum
Paul Storr for Rundell, Bridge &
Rundell
London, 1816
42.5cm (16¾in)
In 1744 both John le Sage[65] and
George Wickes[66] produced
candelabra similar to this design.
They are based on those
illustrated in no.270.

270 A pair of silver candelabra
London, 1738
Charles Frederick Kandler
47.8cm (18¾in)
The figures forming the stems
represent Cupid and Psyche and
the bases have masks representing
the Continents within emblems
of the Four Seasons.
   The design of these candelabra
is based on that by Thomas
Germain.[67]

271 A set of four gilded and
patinated bronze candlesticks
Italian or French, *c*1740
The stems of these candlesticks
are formed from term figures
representing the Four Seasons:
Spring with a garland of roses,
Summer with a scythe and sheaf
of corn, Autumn with fruiting
vines, Winter shown shivering in a
hooded cloak.
   The theme of the Four Seasons
was a popular one and the source
for this design is difficult to
determine with any exactitude.
They are similar to the four in
marble sculpted by François
Coudray (1678–1727) for the
Grosser Garten in Dresden, only
known from Lindemann's
engravings of them.[68] Also similar
are the four in the park at
Versailles[69] which have the same
traditional attributes as the four
illustrated here. Either of these
groups could have been used as a
source for the present group.

269

270

271

272

272 A pair of gilded and
patinated bronze candelabra
French, *c*1740
28cm (11in)

273 A pair of silver candlesticks
London, 1693
Anthony Nelme

*(The Governor and Company of the
Bank of England)*

274 A pair of gilded bronze
candlesticks
English, *c*1770
30.5cm (12in)

(Brand Inglis Ltd)

275 A pair of silver candlesticks
London, 1752
Robert Tyrell

(Brand Inglis Ltd)

[65] Christie's, London, 24 October 1990, lot 247

[66] Elaine Barr, *George Wickes*, London, 1980, fig.42

[67] See a pair of 1734 in the Espirito Santo collection, Portugal.
One is also shown in the portrait of Germain and his wife by
Largillière

[68] François Souchal, *French Sculptors of the 17th and 18th
Centuries*, 1977, p.129

[69] Published by Thomassin, *Receuil des figures, groupes,
thermes, fontaines, vases, statues et autres ornamens de
Versailles*, 1695

273

274

275

276

277

278

279

276 A silver candlestick
London, 1770
Thomas Heming
36.2cm (14¼in)

277 A silver candlestick
London, 1770
Thomas Heming
31.2cm (12¼in)
Engraved with the arms of Henry,
8th Baron Arundell of Wardour
(1740–1808), who rebuilt
Wardour Castle, Wiltshire, from
1770. Objects commissioned for
the house and chapel included
sanctuary lamps from Luigi
Valadier (see no.254).
    This design was used by
Heming for the candlesticks in a
toilet service made in 1768 for Sir
Watkin Williams-Wynn, 4th Bt.
(1749–89), to celebrate his
marriage to Lady Henrietta
Somerset, daughter of the Duke
of Beaufort.[70] The service is
similar to another Heming made,
in 1768, for George III's sister
Caroline, Queen of Denmark.[71]

278 A gilded bronze candlestick
English, *c*1770. 32.5cm (12¾in)

279 A creamware candlestick, in
the white
English (probably Leeds), late
18th century. 28cm (11in)

[70] Now in the National Museum of Wales, see
'The Williams-Wynn silver in the National
Museum of Wales', *Connoisseur*, September
1973

[71] Now in the Kunstindustrimuseum,
Copenhagen

Porcelain candelabra became much more elaborate in the second half of the eighteenth century as the modellers became more adept and the firing techniques more efficient. Again, the human figure seemed the most popular subject.

280

280 A porcelain candlestick figure
English (Longton Hall), *c*1753–54
30cm (11¾in)

281 A three-light porcelain candelabrum
Meissen, mid-18th century
30cm (11¾in)
Modelled as Winter from a set of the Four Seasons, interestingly shown holding a candle lantern.

282 A porcelain three-light candelabrum
Meissen, mid-18th century
Probably by Eberlein
30.3cm (12in)
Modelled as Diana.

283 A pair of porcelain candelabra
Meissen, *c*1745
26.5cm (10½in)
Depicting rustic figures, gardeners and children.

284 A bronze and gilded bronze candelabrum
French, *c*1740

285 A porcelain candlestick group
English (Bow), *c*1765
27cm (10½in)
With figures of Harlequin and Columbine.

286 A porcelain candelabrum
Meissen, mid-18th century
Modelled in the manner of J.J. Kaendler
24.7cm (9¾in)

281/282

283

284

285

286

287 A porcelain candlestick
figure
English (Worcester), 1770-80
22cm (8½in)
Of a gardener.

288 A porcelain candlestick
group
English (Longton Hall), *c*1755
21.3cm (8½in)
Modelled with two putti and a
goat.

289 A porcelain, gilded bronze
and lacquer bougeoir d'accroche
French, mid-18th century
Typical of the objects sold by the
'marchands merciers' (see
no.306) in Paris in the mid-18th
century, this object combines a
porcelain figure and flowers,
probably from the Meissen
factory, with a Chinese lacquer
dish, mounted in gilded bronze
to form a hanging candlestick to
fix on the top of a screen. The
circular rack at the feet of the
porcelain figure is to hold a
snuffer, now missing.

290 A pair of porcelain
candlestick figures
English (Derby), *c*1770
Emblematic of matrimony.

291 A porcelain bocage
candlestick group
English (Chelsea-Derby), *c*1775

(Simon Spero)

292 A pair of porcelain bocage
candlestick groups
English (Chelsea), *c*1765
Emblematic of the Four Seasons.

287

288

289

290

291

292

293 A porcelain-mounted
lacquer and gilded bronze
inkstand
French, mid-18th century
51cm (20in)

294 A pair of gilded bronze and
porcelain candelabra
French, the porcelain Chantilly,
*c*1740
17.5cm (7in)
The chinoiserie figures seated
amid flowers on rocaille bases.

295 A pair of porcelain and
gilded bronze candelabra
the porcelain Meissen, the
mounts French or German,
mid-18th century

293

294

295

308 A glass candelabrum
English, *c*1765

(Brand Inglis Ltd)

309 A glass and gilded bronze
candelabrum
English, *c*1765

(Partridge Fine Art)

310 A gilded bronze
candelabrum
French, *c*1770

311 Design for a candelabrum
French school, *c*1770

(Houthakker collection)

308

309

310

311

312 A gilded bronze, white marble and blue enamel candelabrum
French, *c*1775
56cm (22in)
Conceived as an elaborate vase of carnations, the nozzles concealed in the flowers.

313 A pair of gilded and patinated bronze candelabra
French, *c*1785
95cm (37½in)

314 A pair of gilded bronze, cut-glass, white marble and blue glass candelabra
Baltic, probably Swedish, *c*1790
90cm (35½in)

312

313

314

315 A patinated and gilded bronze
candelabrum with marble base
English, 3rd quarter 18th century
After a design by James Stuart and probably
made by Diederich Nicolaus Andersen or
Matthew Boulton
The original design for candelabra of this
model, and there are several other versions,[72]
has traditionally been attributed to Robert
Adam (mainly on the basis of drawings in the
Soane Museum) and their manufacture, for
want of an alternative, to Matthew Boulton. It
is clear from Sir Nicholas Goodison's
research[73] that the design must originate with
James 'Athenian' Stuart, one of the earliest
practitioners of the Neo-classical style, using
as a basis his sketches of the Choragic
Monument of Lysicrates, later incorporated
into the first volume of Stuart and Revett's
Antiquities of Athens (1762).

It is also clear that the earlier tripods dating
from the 1760s (eg those made for Kedleston
and Spencer House), cannot have been made
by Boulton, since the Boulton factory at Soho
was not equipped to produce this type of
object until the very end of that decade.
Nicholas Goodison proposes the metalworker
Diederich Nicolaus Andersen (d.1767) as a
probable maker for the Curzon, Spencer and
Rockingham tripods, and suggests that
Boulton acquired, probably from Andersen's
widow, either the design or an actual tripod,
from which the later versions (eg Earl
Gower's) were made. These differ slightly in
some details of design. The earliest mention of
Boulton's own tripods seems to be in the sale
of 'Superb and Elegant Produce of Mess.
Boulton and Fothergill's Or Moulu
Manufactory' held at Christie's on 11 April
1771 and two days following, where four are
listed and described as 'after a design of Mr
Stuart's'.

The set of four ordered by Lord Gower
were the subject of a letter from John Hodges,
clerk of the Soho Manufactory, to Matthew
Boulton on 23 April 1777: 'His Lordship
ordered 28 March 4 gilt tripods with marble
plinths and said they must be sent in six weeks
or sooner'. When delivered six *months* later on
23 October the firm declared that they were
'quite at a loss how to apologise for the length
of time taken in compleating these vases' and
enclosed an invoice for £181.1s.6d.

315

316 A silver candelabrum
London, 1774
John Carter
37.5cm (14¾in)
One of a set of four made to a design of
Robert Adam, dated 9 March 1773[74] for Sir
Watkin Williams Wynn. Adam designed a
house for him at 20 St James's Square,
London, in the early 1770s, and several pieces
of silver of comparable quality have survived.[75]
The drawing varies in several details from the
finished object.

(Lloyds of London)

316

---

[72] A pair made for Spencer House, *c*1760 and others at
Kedleston Hall, Wentworth Woodhouse, and a set of four
made for the 2nd Earl Gower, father of 1st Duke of
Sutherland (sold Christie's, 23 November 1972, lot 84)

[73] N.Goodison, 'Mr Stuart's Tripod', *Burlington Magazine*,
October 1972

[74] In the Sir John Soane Museum, London, ill. in Robert
Rowe, *Adam Silver*, London, 1965, pl.13

[75] Including a toilet service, Thomas Heming, 1768, a punch
bowl, Thomas Heming, 1771 (National Museum of Wales), a
pair of sauceboats, John Carter, 1773 (Victoria & Albert
Museum)

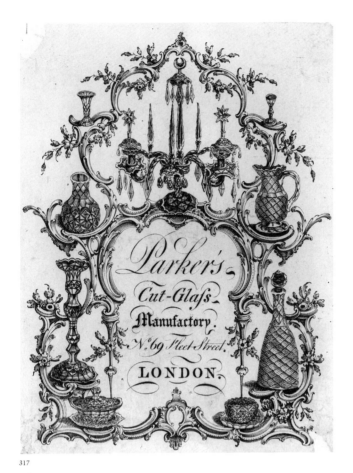

317

318

317 Trade card for Parker's
cut-glass manufactory, no.69
Fleet Street, London
The firm continued, under
various titles, until the 20th
century (see nos 447 and 587).

*(Trustees of the Victoria & Albert
Museum, London)*

318 Trade card for Colebron
Hancock
Glass Manufacturer
'Manufactures and Sells, all Sorts
of Glass, Wholesale, Retail and
for Exportation'.

*(Trustees of the Victoria & Albert
Museum, London)*

The Abbé called them in the evening to attend the
exequies of Mignon. The company proceeded to the Hall
of the Past: they found it magnificently ornamented and
illuminated. The walls were hung with azure tapestry
almost from ceiling to floor, so that nothing but the friezes
and socles, above and below, were visible. On the four
candelabra in the corner wax-lights were burning: smaller
lights were in the four smaller candelabras placed by the
sarcophagus in the middle.

GOETHE, *Wilhelm Meister's Apprenticeship*, 1777–1829; trans. by
Thomas Carlyle

319

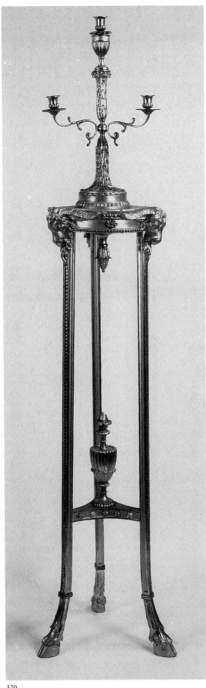

320

321

319 Design for a torchère for Osterley Park
Robert Adam

(Trustees of the Victoria & Albert Museum, London)

320 A gilded wood and gesso torchère, the
candelabrum with gilded metal branches
English, *c*1788
196cm (6ft 5in)
The base of the candelabrum inscribed in
pencil underneath 'September 22nd 1788'.
Made originally for Langley Park, Norfolk.

(Phillips)

321 A gilded bronze and blued metal
candelabrum
French, *c*1780
Attributed to L-F. Feuchère
113.7cm (3ft 8¾in)

*(Now in the J. Paul Getty Museum, Malibu; formerly
in the Mentmore collection)*

322

322 A pair of marble and gilded bronze standing candelabra
French, *c*1780
Signed: J.J. Foucou
133.5cm (4ft 4½in)
In 1779 Foucou exhibited at the Salon two torchères.[76] They were
probably plaster models, as he indicated that they were to be executed
in marble for the Salon of the duchesse de Mazarin.

323

323 A gilded bronze, white marble and porphyry candelabrum
French
Signed:Joan Fr Lorta Sculp. 1788
142cm (4ft 8in)
A set of four candelabra almost identical, the figures representing the
Four Seasons and also bearing the signature of Jean-François Lorta
(1752–88) was made for the Grand Salon at the château of Bellevue for
the aunts of Louis XVI.[77] See also no.729.

324

324 Designs for the decoration
of a room
French school, 1770–80
Showing candelabra similar to
those in the previous illustrations.

(Houthakker collection)

[76] Cat. no.244

[77] Now in the Louvre, cat. no.356

325

325 A silver centrepiece
London, 1780
James Young
46.5cm (18¼in)

328 A marble, gilded bronze and glass
standing lantern
English, *c*1775
180cm (5ft 11in)

327

326 A Blue John, glass and gilded bronze
candlestick
English, *c*1775
Attributed to Matthew Boulton
23cm (9in)

327 A pair of Derbyshire Spa candlesticks
with silver mounts
Probably English, late 18th century, the
mounts with later French control marks
25.5cm (10in)

326

328

329 Design for a candelabrum
English, *c*1770
This drawing has a wonderful
green marbled background. The
candelabrum is very much in the
manner of Matthew Boulton.

*(Trustees of the Victoria & Albert
Museum, London)*

330 A gilded bronze and white
marble candelabrum
English, *c*1770
Attributed to Matthew Boulton
40.5cm (16in)
Boulton (1728–1809) had
workshops in Birmingham where
he executed silverware and fine
objects in gilded bronze and
hardstone, the mounts often after
designs by Adam or Flaxman.
Josiah Wedgwood mentions in a
letter: 'Mr Boulton is, I believe,
the first and most complete
manufacturer in England in
metal. He is very ingenious,
philosophical and agreeable.'

329

331 A gilded bronze
candelabrum
English, *c*1770
35.5cm (14in)

330

331

332a

332b

332 A Sheffield Plate
candelabrum
English, *c*1785
Attributed to Matthew Boulton
54.5cm (21½in)

(Hancocks and Co.)

333

334

335

333 A silver candlestick
Birmingham, 1773
Matthew Boulton and John
Fothergill
29.8cm (11¾in)
Matthew Boulton was
instrumental in the opening of an
assay office in Birmingham in
1773. At the Soho Manufactory,
he employed between 600 and
700 workers, producing silver
and Sheffield Plate as well as
'toys' and ormolu.

334 Plate from a pattern book
English, late 18th century
Matthew Boulton

*(Trustees of the Victoria & Albert
Museum, London)*

335 Candlestick from a pattern
book
English, late 18th century
Matthew Boulton

*(Trustees of the Victoria & Albert
Museum, London)*

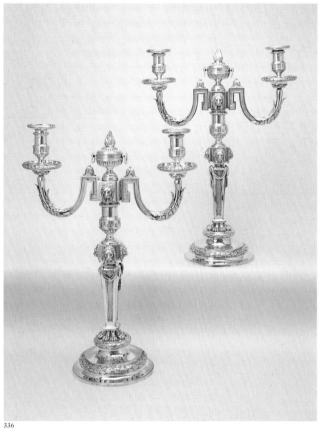

336

337

336 A pair of silver candelabra
London, 1805/6
William Pitts
46.5cm (18¼in)
Like the candelabra of no.270,
this was a design popular with
English silversmiths, though
based on a French original. A pair
by Richard Cooke, 1806, have
central vase-shaped finials, which
are closer to those in Matthew
Boulton's pattern book.[78]
Thomas Heming and Benjamin
Laver made several examples from
1769 to the early 1790s (the
examples illustrated here have
nozzles by Laver) though
Frederick Kandler preceded them
with a set of four in 1765.[79] It is
interesting to see that these
candelabra have identical central
urns to those of no.349.

[78] Michael Snodin, 'Matthew Boulton's
Sheffield Plate Catalogues', *Apollo*, July 1987

[79] Philippa Glanville, *Silver in England*,
London, 1987, p.245

338

337 A gilded bronze candlestick
French or English, c1775
42cm (16½in)
Although almost certainly of
French origin, the only extant
design which this candlestick
follows in much of its detail is
English, from Boulton and
Fothergill's pattern book I, p.41.
The design is for a silver
candlestick but Matthew Boulton
also produced objects in gilded
bronze. The interesting questions
which arise are whether the
design was copied from a French
original or whether the French
copied the Boulton and
Fothergill design.

338 Design for a candlestick
English, late 18th century
From Boulton and Fothergill's
pattern book I, p.41

339 A pair of gilded bronze
candlesticks
French, c1775
28cm (11in)

340 A gilded bronze
candelabrum
French, c1780
50.2cm (19¾in)

341 A gilded wood torchère
French, c1770
176cm (5ft 9½in)

339/340

341

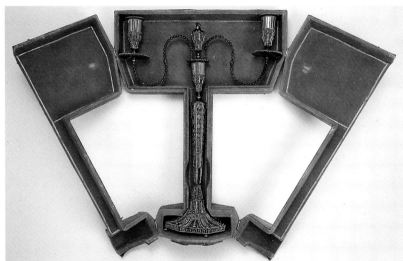

342

342 A cut-steel candelabrum Russian (Tula), late 18th century 47cm (18½in) In its original fitted red leather case.

This was originally one of a pair of candelabra given in the late 18th century to Goya's famous patroness, the Duchess of Alba. Tula had long been famed for its arms and armour when the factory was extended in 1712 to produce domestic objects including even furniture. The products of the factory were highly prized and extraordinarily expensive in their day and Catherine II often gave pieces to foreign royalty and dignitaries as presents.

343

344

345

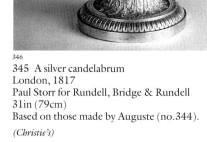

346

343 Design for a torchère or
candlestick stem
Jean-Charles Delafosse
(1734–89)
Architect, designer and professor
of drawing, Delafosse published
his *Nouvelle Iconologie Historique*
in 1768 with an enlarged second
edition in 1771. The work
contained numerous designs for
furniture, trophies etc. all in Neo-
classical style.

(Houthakker collection)

344 A silver four-light
candelabrum
Paris, 1780
Robert-Joseph Auguste
56cm (22in)
One of four candelabra, part of a
service made for George III of
England (r.1760–1820),
between 1776 and 1785,
probably for use at
Herrenhausen. The candlesticks
in the service, by Frantz Peter
Bunsen of Hanover, *c*1794, did
not include caryatid figures in the
design. Auguste used a variant of
the three female figures in
another service, made for Count
Creutz when Swedish
Ambassador to Paris, in
1775/76.[80]

*(Now in the J.Paul Getty Museum,
Malibu)*

[80] In the Royal Palace, Stockholm

345 A silver candelabrum
London, 1817
Paul Storr for Rundell, Bridge & Rundell
31in (79cm)
Based on those made by Auguste (no.344).

(Christie's)

346 A gilded bronze candelabrum
French, *c*1780
After a design by Jean-Démosthène Dugourc
62.5cm (24¾in)
In the late 1780s an album of designs was
compiled for Madame Elisabeth and the
comte de Provence, probably by Dugourc.
The album[81] contains a design for a
candlestick identical to this one, without its
branches. Dugourc (1749–1825) was named
in 1780 as dessinateur du cabinet de Monsieur
(the comte de Provence).

Nos 349–352 demonstrate the way in which a design was adapted, often in only
very minor details, to produce a variant to a popular model.

The original design is based on a pair of candelabra by Robert-Joseph Auguste,
Paris, 1766–67, at Woburn Abbey.[82] Goldsmiths whose marks appear on these candlesticks include Andrew Fogelberg and John Römer, both of Scandinavian origin,
also Benjamin Laver and Thomas Heming, who appear to have had a business as-
sociation, the latter being appointed Royal Goldsmith in 1760.

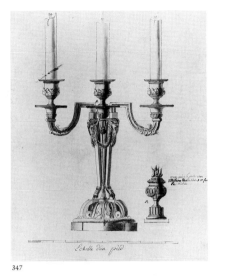

347

348

349

350

351

352

347 Design for a candelabrum
French school, *c*1775

348 Design for a candelabrum
French, late 18th century
Attributed to Robert-Joséph Auguste

[81] Now at the Musée des Arts Décoratifs, Paris

[82] Arthur Grimwade, 'Family Silver of three Centuries', *Apollo*, December 1965

[83] Christie's, London, 17/18 March 1987, lots 390 and 391

349 A silver candelabrum
London, 1771
Candlestick: John Römer; branches: Thomas Heming
36.3cm (14¼in)
This variant, without the rams' heads, was also made by John Römer in 1769 and by Andrew Fogelberg in 1774 (see no.222).[83]

(Christie's)

350 A silver candlestick
Paris, 1782
Robert-Joseph Auguste

351 A silver candelabrum
London, 1780/83
38cm (15in)
From a set of six, of which two candlesticks and one branch were marked by Benjamin Laver 1783, four candlesticks by George Heming and William Chawner 1780, and three branches by Thomas Heming 1780.

352 A silver candelabrum
London, 1781
Benjamin Laver
38.5cm (15¼in)

353

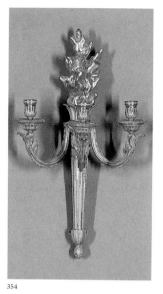

354

355

356

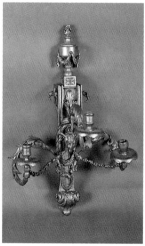

357

358

359

360

353 Design for a wall-light
Jean-Louis Prieur or Richard de Lalonde
On which no.354 is based.

(Now in the J. Paul Getty Museum, Malibu)

354 A gilded bronze wall-light
Paris, c1775
66cm (26in)
This is thought to be part of a large group of wall-lights, all of the same basic design, delivered for use in the Royal palaces from about 1775.[84] No.353 shows a design for a two-branch wall-light very similar to this pair.

355 A gilded wood wall-light
Dutch, probably Haarlem, in the manner of Hans Pieter Nijborg (c1736–1806), late 18th century
63.5cm (25in)
Possibly based on the design in no.353

356 A gilded bronze wall-light
French, c1760
Probably by Pierre-Philippe Caffieri
58.5cm (13in)
Caffieri supplied wall-lights of similar design, only known from contemporary descriptions,[85] for Louis XV's hunting lodge, Saint-Hubert. Descriptions of similar

items also appear in the inventory taken of Caffieri's stock in 1770.

357 A gilded wood wall-light
Italian, c1775
80cm (27in)

358 A gilded bronze wall-light
Dutch, c1775
33cm (13in)
Reputedly made for the Palace of Buitenzorg, one of the residences of the Prince of Orange.

359 A gilded bronze wall-light
French, c1780
75cm (29½in)

360 A gilded bronze wall-light
French, c1785
39cm (15¼in)

[84]There is an identical pair in the château de Fontainebleau and another in the J. Paul Getty Museum, Malibu

[85] *Journal de l'Agriculture, du Commerce, des Arts et des Finances,* December 1771, which describes in detail the furnishings of the château de Saint-Hubert

361 A pair of gilded bronze wall-lights
French, *c*1775
In the manner of Pitoin
50cm (19¾in)

361

362

363

362 A gilded and painted wood and plaster
wall-light
English, *c*1775

363 A gilded wood and plaster wall-light
English, *c*1775
61cm (24in)

364 A gilded and painted wood and plaster
wall-light
English, *c*1790

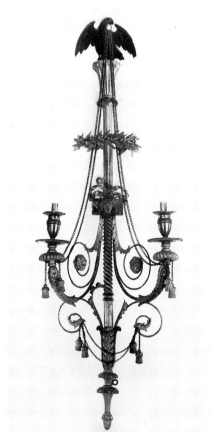

364

365 A cut-glass chandelier
English, *c*1770
127cm (4ft 2in)

366 A gilded bronze chandelier
French, *c*1780

(Musée Nissim de Camondo, Paris)

367 The Prodigal Son revelling with Harlots
Amos Doolittle (1754–1832)
Published and sold by Shelton & Kensett,
Cheshire, Connecticut, Oct 24 1814
Amos Doolittle was one of the earliest
American engravers on copper.
   The louche company is revelling in the light
of a wall girandole in the style of the 1780s.

(The American Museum in Britain, Bath)

368 Design for a mirror
English, late 18th century
John Yenn (1750–1821)
Yenn was the pupil and assistant of the
architect Sir William Chambers.

(Trustees of the Victoria & Albert Museum, London)

365

366

The PRODIGAL SON revelling with HARLOTS

367

368

113

369

369 Detail of the central panel of
a tapestry
Gobelins factory, 1771–73
Given by Louis XVI in 1786 to
the Duke and Duchess of Saxe-
Teschen.
   The scene shows Sancho Panza
feasting on the Isle of Barataria,
and is after a painting by Charles-
Antoine Coypel, in the château de
Compiègne.

370 A cut- and mirror-glass
girandole wall-light
Irish, late 18th century
90cm (35½in)

371 A gilded wood girandole
wall-light
Italian, c1780
89cm (35in)

372 A glass wall-light
English, c1780
56cm (22in)

370

371

372

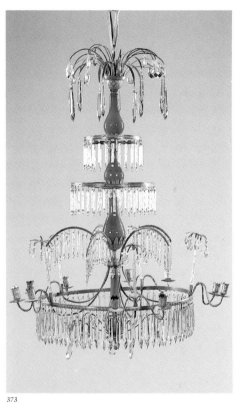

373

374

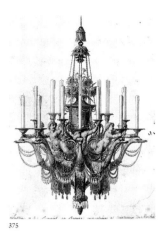

375

376

377

373 A cut-glass, opaline glass and gilt-metal chandelier
Russian, *c*1790
107cm (3ft 6in)

374 A cut-glass and gilt-metal chandelier
English, *c*1780
(Malletts)

375 Design for a chandelier
Jean-Démosthène Dugourc (1749–1825)
To be executed in bronze, porcelain and rock-crystal.
(Houthakker collection)

376 A gilded bronze, cut-glass and blue glass chandelier
Swedish, *c*1790
122cm (4ft)

377 A gilded-bronze and glass chandelier
Scandinavian or Russian, *c*1795
100cm (3ft 3½in)

378

379

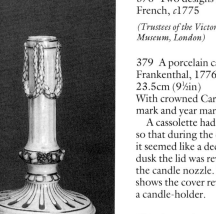

380

381

382

378 Two designs for candlesticks
French, *c*1775

(Trustees of the Victoria & Albert Museum, London)

379 A porcelain cassolette
Frankenthal, 1776
23.5cm (9½in)
With crowned Carl Theodor mark and year mark for 1776.
   A cassolette had a reversible lid so that during the daylight hours it seemed like a decorative vase; at dusk the lid was reversed to reveal the candle nozzle. The illustration shows the cover reversed for use as a candle-holder.

380 A porcelain candlestick
Hochst, 1775-80
18cm (7in)

381 A silver candlestick
Paris, 1784
Jean-Charles Duchaine
28cm (11in)

382 A gilded and patinated bronze candlestick
French, *c*1785
In the form of a cannon held up by three putti.

383 A pair of bronze, gilded bronze and marble candlesticks
French, *c*1785
28cm (11in)

384 A pair of bronze, gilded bronze, enamel and marble candlesticks
French, late 18th century
33cm (13in)

383

384

385

386

385 Four silver candlesticks
Sheffield, 1775
Maker's mark overstruck by John
Carter of London; one nozzle:
John Parsons & Co.,Sheffield
30.2cm (12in)
These are typical of many
candlesticks made in Sheffield at
this time: made of thin sheet silver
with die-stamped decoration and
filled with pitch to give strength
and stability. John Carter was an
important maker of candlesticks
in London (see no.316) but,
judging from the quantity of
candlesticks which survive with
his mark overstriking others,
obviously bought extensively
from Sheffield makers to add to
his stock.

386 A pair of silver candlesticks
London, 1777
Robert Makepiece and Richard
Carter
23.5cm (9¼in)

387 A silver candlestick
Rotterdam, 1779
Rudolph Sondag
24.5cm (9¾in)

388 A silver candlestick
Flemish (Malines), 1795
28.5cm (11¼in)

389 A silver candlestick
The Hague, 1782
Martinus van Stapele
24cm (9½in)

387

388

389

390

391

390 A pair of Sheffield Plate
candlesticks
English, *c*1785

(Brand Inglis Ltd)

391 Design for a candlestick
English, late 18th century
Signed: R.M.

*(Trustees of the Victoria & Albert
Museum, London)*

392 Ten silver-gilt candlesticks
London, 1776
Thomas Heming
28.5cm (11¼in)
Probably from the service of plate
provided by Catherine II for the
Governors of the province of Tula
in Russia, famous for its work in
cut-steel (see no.342). The
service included thirty-eight
candlesticks together with salvers,
meat dishes and dinner plates.
Arthur Grimwade[86] quotes
Gottfried Lichterberg writing
about a service assumed to be this
one: 'A silver service worth
30,000 pounds has been ordered
from the famous silversmith in
Bond Street Mr Hemins some
days ago. It will go abroad and
even he does not know the
recipient. He makes it on the
order of two City merchants.'

392

393 Four silver candlesticks
Paris, 1771
Jacques-Nicolas Roettiers
32.2cm (12¾in)
Part of the service of
approximately three thousand
pieces ordered by Catherine the
Great in 1770 and given to Prince
Gregory Orloff. The commission
was received by J-N. Roettier and
completed with the aid of his
father, Edmé-Pierre Balzac,
Louis-Joseph Lenhendrick and
others. Prince Orloff died in
1783, when the service was re-
acquired by Catherine.

393

[86] Arthur Grimwade, *London Goldsmiths
1697–1837*, 3rd edn, London, 1976

394 A gilded bronze candlestick
French, *c*1780
21cm (8¼in)
The draped female heads possibly
represent Winter.

395 A gilded bronze candlestick
French, *c*1770
23.5cm (9¼in)

396 A pair of cut-glass, gilded
brass and Wedgwood candlesticks
English, *c*1790
33cm (13in)

397 A gilded bronze and bleu
turquin marble candlestick
French, *c*1785
34.5cm (13½in)

398 Entrance Hall, Lythwood
English, *c*1780
G.Stewart
A wonderful naive representation
of an entrance hall with a pair of
wall-lights, perhaps with oval
glass panels or all in gilded wood,
and a small chandelier.

The chandelier appears to hang
from a chain which disappears
through a small hole at the centre
of the ceiling rose. Could there be
a concealed pulley system above
for raising and lowering the
chandelier when the candles
needed changing? It seems
unlikely, as there would have to
be enough space to allow for the
compensating weights, but there
appears to be no sign of a hook
for it to hang from.

*(Trustees of the Victoria & Albert
Museum, London)*

399 A glass and gilded metal
candlestick
English, *c*1780
The pedestal base gilt in the
manner of James Giles
31cm (12¼in)

400 A gilded bronze, cut-glass
and Wedgwood candlestick
English, *c*1785
The mounts in the manner of
Matthew Boulton
40.7cm (16in)

399

400

401 John Middleton with his
family in their drawing room
Philip Reinagle, RA
(1749–1833)
John Middleton was an artist's
colourman, who lived at 80 St
Martin's Lane, London. On the
chimney-piece is a pair of
candlesticks hung with glass
drops similar to those shown in
nos 399–400.

401

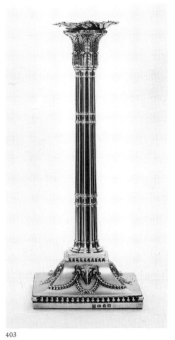

402

403

404

405

406

407

402 A pair of paktong candlesticks
English, c1765
26cm (10¼in)

403 A silver candlestick
Sheffield, 1773
Tudor and Leader

404 A pair of brass candlesticks
English, c1780
31.5cm (12½in)

405 A silver candlestick
Stockholm, 1795
Johan Wilhelm Zimmerman
27cm (10½in)

406 A creamware candlestick, in the white
English (possibly Whitehead), c1800
26cm (10¼in)

407 A silver-lustre candlestick
English (Leeds), c1810
23cm (9in)

408/409/410

411

412

413

408 A pair of white marble, gilded and
patinated bronze candlesticks
English, early 19th century, 43 cm (17in)
These candlesticks are taken from an etching
by Charles Heathcote Tatham (1722–1842).[87]
The signed etching is inscribed: *Antique
Chimera in basso relievo of white marble, a
fragment at Rome* and *Published May 1798 by
C.H. Tatham London.*
Because of their similarity to no.412 they
were perhaps made by Benjamin Lewis
Vulliamy.

409 A pair of hardstone and gilded bronze
cassolettes
English, *c*1790, 20cm (8in)
In the illustration the lid is shown reversed on
one of the cassolettes. The different decorative
stones and materials used on these pieces are
(from the top downwards): lavender-coloured
opaque glass, jasper, quartz, jasper (possibly
silicified and iron-stained volcanic ash),
banded volcanic ash (silicified), green
rhydolite, quartz, buff iron-stained quartzite,
silicified wood.

410 A bronze and tôle adjustable lamp,
sometimes known as a student's lamp
English, *c*1820
Signed by Miller & Son, Piccadilly
50cm (19¾in)

411 A pair of porcelain
candlesticks
English (Derby), late 18th century
21cm (8¼in)

412 A pair of patinated and
gilded bronze candlesticks
English
Signed B. Vulliamy and dated
1811
On slate bases.
Benjamin Lewis Vulliamy
(1780–1854), worked at 74 Pall
Mall, London, from 1807 to
1816. He probably based these
candlesticks on a design by
Charles Heathcote Tatham, see
no.408.

413 Design for a sphinx
candlestick
John Yenn (1750–1821)[88]

*(Trustees of the Victoria & Albert
Museum, London)*

[87] Pl.40 in his first published work *Etchings of
Ancient Ornamental Sculpture drawn from
the Originals in Rome and other parts of Italy
during the years 1794, 1795 and 1797*,
published 1799–1800

[88] For information on Yenn's designs for silver
see 'Sir William Chambers and John Yenn:
designs for silver', *Burlington Magazine*,
January 1986; and 'Sir William Chambers
and the Duke of Marlborough's Silver',
Apollo, June 1987, both by Hilary Young

414

414 A pair of carved ivory
candlesticks
Late 18th/early 19th century
28cm (11in)
In the form of recumbent
sphinxes. These are possibly of
Anglo-Indian origin, though
seem close, also, to French
models in gilded bronze which
are in turn traditionally supposed
to be inspired by designs done by
Nicolas Coustou[89] for lead
sphinxes to stand on the terrace
of the Royal Pavilion at Marly.

415 A porcelain candlestick
English (Worcester), *c*1810–13
Barr, Flight & Barr.
In the form of a griffin seated on a
rectangular base painted with a
bullfinch.

[89] Two designs are conserved in the Cabinet
of Drawings in the Stockholm Museum

415

The spout lamp, which often resembled a teapot, the spout forming the wick-holder and burner, persisted in use from ancient times until well into the nineteenth century. The main fuel was whale oil, changing later to colza or rape seed oil, while in Mediterranean countries olive oil was sometimes used. Hanging lamps of this type often had more than one spout. The *lucernae* of Italy and other Mediterranean countries sometimes had elaborate stands or hanging devices and could be fitted with trimmers, prickers for raising the wicks, tweezers and snuffers, and were the most advanced form of spout lamp (see nos 425–6). The Dutch and Flemish versions often resembled coffee pots (no.437). The spout lamp was certainly of European origin, and the American lamps were based on originals from Germany and Holland.

416

416 Interior with peasants
Johann Georg Trautman
(1713–69)
In this painting the room is lit by
a crusie lamp, similar to the one
shown in no.417.

417 A wrought-iron crusie lamp
18th century
39cm (15½in)
With swivel-action shutter and
iron hanging support.

418 A tin lamp
American or German, 18th
century

(Collection Mr J.W. Blum)

419 A tin lamp
Probably American, 18th century

(Collection Mr J.W. Blum)

420 A 'Betty' lamp
American (New England), early
18th century
With adjustable turned wood
stand. The 'Betty' lamp was an
advancement on the earlier
'Phoebe' lamp, possibly so-called
because it was *better* than the
Phoebe lamp, which had two pans,
one to contain the oil and another
below to catch the precious drips.
The Betty lamp had a wick-holder
fixed to the base of the lamp so
that the drippings from the wick
were fed back into the reservoir.

(The American Museum in Britain, Bath)

417

418

419

420

421

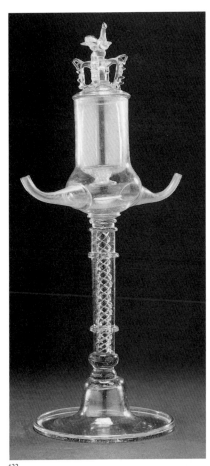

422

421 Design for an oil lamp
French school, *c*1780
(Houthakker collection)

422 A glass lamp
Liège, 18th century
42cm (16½in)

423 Portrait of Madame
Récamier
Jacques-Louis David, begun in
June 1800
Showing an oil lamp in classical
style in bronze, standing on a
bronze torchère.

(Musée du Louvre, Paris)

423

424

425

424 The Hon Mrs Charles
Russell
John Singer Sargent (1856–1925)
Dated 1900
Mrs Russell is standing beside an
Italian silver oil lamp of the late
18th century.

425 A silver lamp
Rome, *c*1825
Angelo Giannotti
56.5cm (22¼in)

426

426 A bronze, silver and marble
lamp
Rome, dated 1814
The silver with the mark of Luigi
Antonio Mattei
40cm (15¾in)

427 Young girl writing a letter
Jan Koelman
This fashionably dressed young
lady of the mid-19th century is
writing her letter by the light of
what must have been by then a
distinctly old-fashioned type of
lamp. These lamps obviously
continued in use well after the
introduction of the more efficient
and much brighter Argand oil
lights.

427

428

429

430

428 A silver oil lamp
Rome, *c*1840
Angelo Giannotti
16cm (6¼in)
This design was also popular in
ceramics. Wedgwood made lamps
in black basalt, entitled 'Reading'
and 'Vestal', from the 1770s
onwards.

429 A porcelain lamp
German (KPM), 2nd quarter
19th century
27cm (10½in)
The Königliche Porzellan
Manufaktur was so named by
Frederick the Great when the
Berlin porcelain factory became a
Royal factory in 1763.

430 A lustreware lamp
English (probably Coalport),
*c*1800-10
24.2cm (9½in)
This lamp, the silver example
(no.428) and the porcelain one
(no.429), all follow the same
basic formula of a classical lamp
surmounted by a kneeling figure
(winged in the other two
examples) filling the lamp from an
ewer of oil. It is possibly inspired
by a design by John Flaxman.[90]

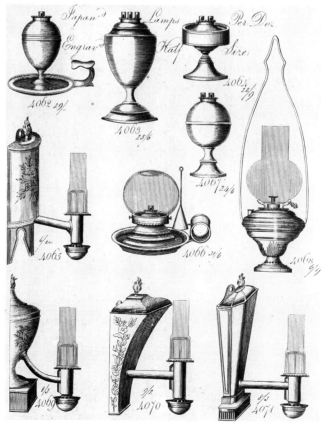

431

431 Plate from a lamp-maker's
catalogue
English, early 19th century

*(Trustees of the Victoria & Albert
Museum, London)*

[90] Design for a teapot, possibly inspired by an
antique lamp, now in the Fitzwilliam
Museum, Cambridge, see *John Flaxman RA,*
exh. cat., Royal Academy of Arts, London,
October–December 1979, ill.23

433

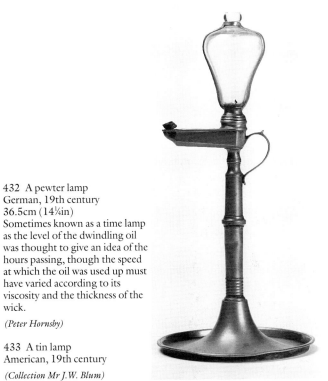

432 A pewter lamp
German, 19th century
36.5cm (14¼in)
Sometimes known as a time lamp
as the level of the dwindling oil
was thought to give an idea of the
hours passing, though the speed
at which the oil was used up must
have varied according to its
viscosity and the thickness of the
wick.

(Peter Hornsby)

433 A tin lamp
American, 19th century

(Collection Mr J.W. Blum)

432

434

435

434 Three glass lamps
18th/early 19th century
27.5cm (10¾in); 19cm (7½in);
23.5cm (9¼in)

435 A brass gimbal light, with
carrying handle
American, 19th century
This type of lamp was designed so
that it could be used either
standing on a table or hanging on
a wall or, indeed, on a boat.

(Collection Mr J.W. Blum)

436 Pewter whale oil lamps
American, 19th century

(Peter Hornsby)

436

437

The Lamp, for work at night, may be of such constructions as . . . best suits the engraver. He can use oil or gas . . . The ordinary light of an oil lamp or single gas-jet is not strong enough for an engraver's work . . . To concentrate and intensify the light of this single burner, either of two things may be used: a hollow glass globe . . . or what is called a 'bulls-eye', a piece of solid glass round on one side and flat on the other, as if it had been cut off a solid globe.'

W.J. LINTON, *Wood engraving, a manual of instruction*, 1884

437 Interior of a cottage at Schiedam, Holland
Mary Ellen Best, dated 16 July 1838
Showing two spout lamps, probably made of tin and of typical coffee-pot form, hanging on the wall.

438 A tin bull's-eye lamp
American, 19th century
The lens was used to concentrate the light onto a book or piece of work.

(Collection Mr J.W. Blum)

439 A pewter double bull's-eye lamp
American, 19th century
Of the type patented by Roswell Gleason
19cm (7½in)

(The American Museum in Britain, Bath)

438

439

440

440 Watercolour of a bedroom
Italian, *c*1840
From the ceiling hangs a bowl
light in either alabaster or white
marble, in classical style.

*(Trustees of the Victoria & Albert
Museum, London)*

441 A bronze hanging lamp
Neapolitan, mid-19th century
Signed: Fonderia Giorgio
Sommer, Via Calabritto 23,
Napoli

442 A painted and cut-glass and
gilded bronze hanging light
Viennese, *c*1825

441

442

In 1783 a Swiss chemist, Ami Argand (1759–1803), invented a burner for oil lamps, known as the Argand burner, which revolutionized their performance. The burner consisted of two concentric tubes surrounding a cotton wick which enabled a double current of air to be drawn up through the wick. Over this was placed a glass chimney to increase the upward draught. This produced a light ten times greater than a candle flame, transforming the activities which could take place after dusk.

In Europe oil lighting was usually fuelled by colza oil, made from the rape seed, an extremely viscous liquid, too thick to be drawn up the wick by capillary action, so the reservoir had to be placed higher than the wick, enabling the oil to run down to it by the force of gravity. Chandeliers either had a main central reservoir which fed all the burners, or sometimes each burner had its individual reservoir. The disadvantage of these lamps was that the reservoir invariably cast a huge shadow.

One of the earliest extant representations of an Argand lamp is the portrait of Dr Alphonse Leroy, by Jacques-Louis David.[91] Painted in 1783, it shows the doctor sitting beside a brass Argand lamp with a glass reservoir of yellowish oil. Both Matthew Boulton (1728–1809) and Josiah Wedgwood (1730–95) produced Argand lamps. Sophie V la Roche, in her diary for 15 September 1786 states: '. . . we finished tea at evening investigating Argand lamps of all descriptions'. She continues to describe the shop in Bedford Street where these lamps were displayed '. . . forming a really dazzling spectacle; every variety . . . crystal, lacquer and metal ones, silver and brass and every possible shade'.

443

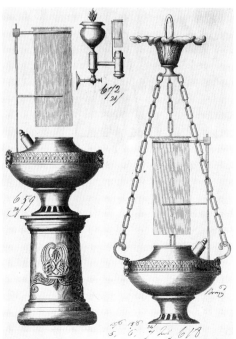

444

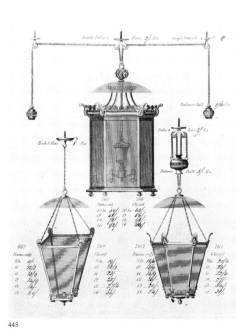

445

443 Design from a chandelier-maker's pattern book
French, early 19th century
Bound with other designs for Morant & Co., 91 New Bond Street. A note with the design tells us that when executed it would cost about £40 gilded and £28 in bronze.

(Trustees of the Victoria & Albert Museum, London)

444 Plate from a catalogue of G.A. Glick
English, early 19th century
Designs for oil burners of unusual form.

(Trustees of the Victoria & Albert Museum, London)

445 Plate from a manufacturer's catalogue
English, early 19th century

(Trustees of the Victoria & Albert Museum, London)

[91] Now in the Musée Fabre, Montpellier

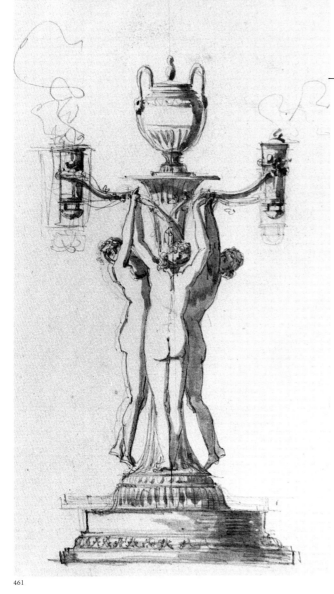

461

462

461 Design for an oil lamp
Italian, late 18th century
Based on a plate in Piranesi's *Vasi
candelabri, cippi, sarcofagi,
tripodi, lucerne ed ornamenti
antichi* (fig.27), showing an
antique marble in the Palazzo
della Villa Borghese in Rome.
The lamp would probably have
been executed in bronze and/or
gilded bronze, perhaps with a
marble base. The original Piranesi
engravings were published
separately from 1768–78 and
then collected together in a two-
volume edition in 1778. The
model was also well-known in
France from etchings by the Abbé
de Saint-Non after Laurent
Guiard (1723–88) who had
drawn the *Three Graces* in Rome
in 1756 and probably provided
inspiration for a whole group of
clocks in marble and gilded
bronze.

(Houthakker collection)

462 A pair of patinated bronze,
gilded brass and glass oil lamps
New York, *c*1835
J. & I. Cox
52cm (20½in)

463 Plate from a manufacturer's
catalogue
English, *c*1825

*(Trustees of the Victoria & Albert
Museum, London)*

463

It was now grown dark. She took him to the Count's
wardrobe, made him change his own coat with his
lordship's silk night-gown, and put the cap with red
trimmings on his head. She then led him forward to the
cabinet; and bidding him sit down upon the large chair
and take a book, she lit the Argand lamp which stood
before him, and showed him what he was to do, and what
kind of part he had to play.

GOETHE, *Wilhelm Meister's Apprenticeship*, 1777–1829; trans. by
Thomas Carlyle.

In 1800 Bernard-Guillaume Carcel invented a clockwork mechanism to raise the oil to the wick, no longer necessitating the reservoir to be higher than the wick. This clockwork pump was improved by Franchot in 1836 when he produced his 'moderator' lamp, which had a spring-loaded piston to give pressure to the fuel. Lamps with complicated mechanisms such as these were expensive and still in 1860 *Cassell's Household Guide* was advising: 'these lamps are liable to get out of order soon and for constant work are not to be compared with the old Argand burners'.

464 Figures in a salon
German school, *c*1825
The chandelier and gaming tables are lit by candles, but between the windows stand a pair of oil lamps of Carcel type, and the wall-lights appear to be oil-fuelled, with Argand burners.

465 Plate from the trade catalogue of Mons. Chopin of 257 rue St Denis, Paris
Early 19th century

(Trustees of the Victoria & Albert Museum, London)

466 A pair of gilded and patinated bronze lamps
French, early 19th century
Each base has a label 'CARCEL, inventeur Breveté, rue de l'arbre sec No.18 à Paris'
97cm (38in)
Bernard-Guillaume Carcel is recorded at the rue de l'Arbre Sec between 1800 and 1812. One of the star-engraved shades has a mid 19th-century Baccarat paper label.

467 A pair of gilded and patinated bronze and marble lamps
French, mid nineteenth century
96.5cm (42in)

468 A pair of gilded opaline glass oil lamps
French, *c*1835
80cm (30½in)

466

467

469 Reception room
Mary Ellen Best
In January 1840 Mary Ellen Best
was married to Johann Anton
Phillip Sarg. This is a watercolour
of the four walls of one of the
reception rooms of the first house
they shared together in Frankfurt,
probably executed in late 1841 or
early 1842. It is one of a set of
three watercolours of the main
rooms in the house. They are
constructed to fold at the corners
and stand up, the three rooms
inter-connecting.

By this time, in an upper-
middle-class home, the column
oil lamp is left standing on the
little side-table, even during the
day.

468

If the patent lamps be lighted up every evening, they
should be emptied once a week. Do not put the oil that
comes from them into the jar with the best oil, but keep it
separate to burn in the common lamps. In the cold
weather warm the oil by putting the lamps near the hall fire
... In frosty weather in particular, the glasses are very easily
broken by sudden transition from cold to heat ... Use
wax-tapers, or matches without brimstone for lighting
them, but not paper ... The smoking of lamps is
frequently disregarded in domestic life: but the fumes
ascending from oil, especially if it be tainted or rancid, are
highly pernicious when inhaled into the lungs of asthmatic
persons.

MACKENZIE's *Five Thousand Receipts*, 4th edn, Philadelphia,
1829, quoted by Major L.B.Wyant, 'The Etiquette of
Nineteenth-Century Lamps', *Antiques*, September 1936

469

In the late eighteenth and early nineteenth century there were no leaps forward in technique in the craft of the candle-maker as there had been in the art of the lamp-maker. Luckily for the chandlers, oil lamps, especially Argand lamps, were comparatively expensive. The bills and cards here illustrated show that the chandler's wares were, spermaceti apart, much the same as they had been one hundred years earlier, though some candle-makers had branched out into selling soap, starch and bleach, as well as light-fittings.

470

471

470 Trade card of George Prior, wax and tallow chandler
English, 1808
Like many chandlers, George Prior sold soap, starch and blues in addition to supplying wax and tallow (or mould) candles

(Trustees of the British Museum, London)

471 A candle box
English, 1st half 19th century
Tallow candles tended to rot if they were exposed to the air for too long. In some places they were buried in bran to preserve them, but more usually they were stored in special boxes, often wall-hanging, made of either wood, brass or, as in the illustrated example, tin-plate.

(Museum of English Rural Life, Reading)

472

473

472 A fruitwood candle-stand
Early 19th century
23cm (9in)

473 Trade card of Glossops
English, 1814
Engraved by T. Hunter, Frith Street, Soho
'Elegant Chandaliers & Lamps of all Descriptions, let on Hire, for Concerts, Routs & Illuminations; The Lighting of Public Offices, Theatres, Parishes &c contracted for on the lowest mercantile Price'. The British Museum also holds an account from F. Glossop dated 1817 for wax, spermaceti and composition candles.

(Trustees of the British Museum, London)

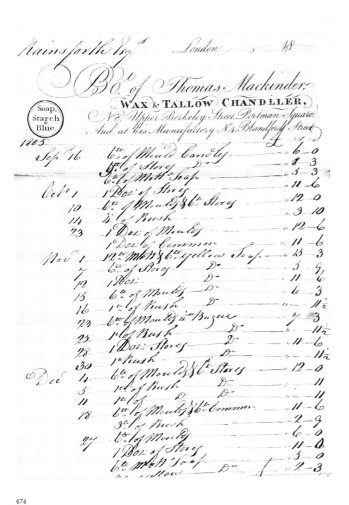

474

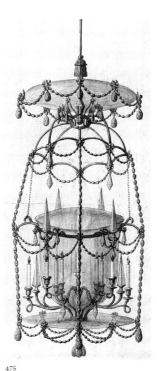

475

474 Account from Thomas Mackinder to – Rainsforth Esqr
English, dated 1805
The bill lists a variety of lighting material, some sold by weight, some by the dozen as well as soap. It includes, for example:
  6 lb of Mould Candles
  4 lb of Rush
  1 Doz of Common
  1 Doz of Store

(Trustees of the British Museum, London)

475 Design for a glass and gilt-metal lantern
English, *c*1790
The elaborate brass or gilded bronze frame hung with glass drops.

(Trustees of the Victoria & Albert Museum, London)

476

476 Interior scene
Northern European or Russian, *c*1825
The interior is rather simple in its fittings except for the two monumental stoves and the very grand lantern. This probably dates from the latter years of the 18th century and is festooned with glass or rock-crystal drops.

(Trustees of the Victoria & Albert Museum, London)

477

478

479

477 Interior: a drawing room
Mary Ellen Best
Showing an English glass chandelier typical of the early years of the 19th century.

478 The Piccadilly Drawing Room, Apsley House, London
early 19th century
The chandelier is close to the design in no.479 and may have been supplied by Hancock, Rixon & Dunt.

(Trustees of the Victoria & Albert Museum, London)

479 Design for a chandelier
English, *c*1810
For Hancock, Rixon & Dunt
Very similar to pieces supplied for Apsley House, see no.478. This design seems still to have been current at the time of the Great Exhibition in 1851.

(Trustees of the Victoria & Albert Museum, London)

480

481

482

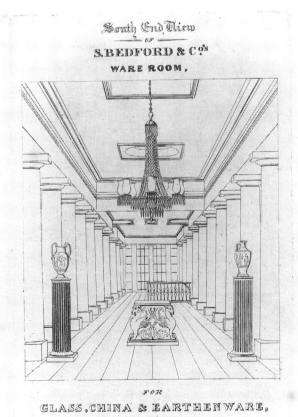

483

480 A cut-glass and gilded brass
chandelier
English, *c*1805
175cm (5ft 9in)

481 A cut-glass and gilded
bronze chandelier
English, *c*1825

*(Spencer House Ltd, photograph
Lucinda Lambton)*

482 A cut-glass and gilt-metal
chandelier
English, early 19th century
198cm (6ft 5in)

483 Advertisement from *The
History, Topography and Directory
of Warwickshire*
English, published 1835

(Private collection)

484

485

486

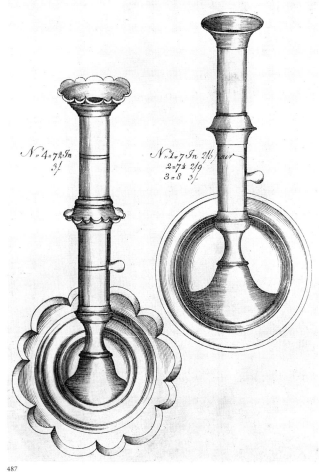
487

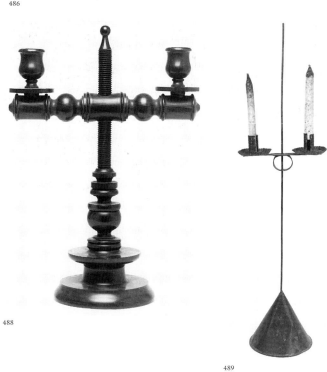
488

490

489

484 A porcelain candlestick
English (Worcester), c1800
Flight and Barr
16.5cm (6½in)
One of a pair painted on a yellow
ground with classical figures
emblematic of War and Peace.

485 A pair of telescopic Sheffield
Plate candlesticks
English, c1800

(Hancocks & Co.)

486 A pair of porcelain
candlesticks
English, c1810–25

(Simon Spero)

487 Engraved design for brass
candlesticks
English, late 18th century
From a bound volume containing
also designs for sugar casters,
handbells, etc.

(Trustees of the Victoria & Albert
Museum, London)

488 A lignum vitae candelabrum
19th century
39cm (15¼in)

489 A tin two-branch candle-
holder
American, 19th century

(Collection Mr J.W. Blum)

490 A brass candlestick, with
reflecting panel
English, early 19th century
51cm (20in)

491 Le Soir ou les apprêts du bal
French engraving, early 19th
century
Showing a young lady dressing
before her cheval-glass with
candle-arms.

(Private collection)

491

492 A pair of silver candlesticks
Paris, 1809
Jean-Baptiste-Claude Odiot
Odiot (1763–1850) retired in 1827, and the
firm was then run by his son, Charles.

493 Catalogue of G.A. Glick
English, early 19th century
The scrolling wires beneath the nozzles on the
four outside candlesticks are to take pendant
glass drops.

(Trustees of the Victoria & Albert Museum, London)

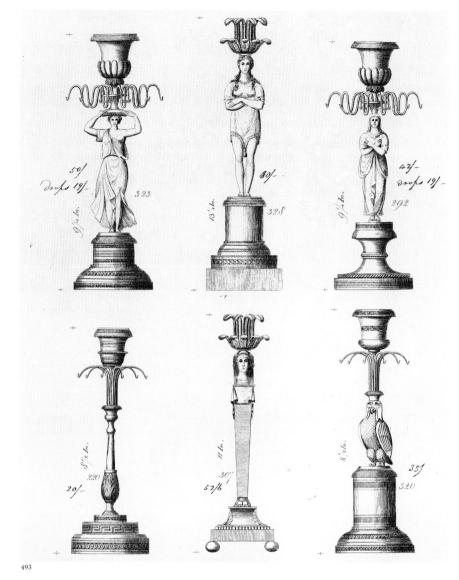

492

493

494

495

496

494 A patinated and gilded
bronze candlestick
French, early 19th century
28cm (11in)

495 A cut-glass and gilded
bronze candlestick
French, *c*1820
28cm (11in)
Mme Desarnaud Charpentier, de
Bougarel, Bucher and Falateuf
were all artisans who had
boutiques in the Palais Royal and
who are recorded dealing in
objects of cut-glass with gilded
bronze mounts.

496 A silver candlestick
Copenhagen, 1825
Pierre Frontin
28.5cm (11¼in)

497

498

497 Two pairs of gilded bronze and malachite candelabra
Russian, early 19th century
77.5cm and 103cm (30½in and 40½in)
Because of the schistic nature of malachite it is impossible to use it in block form and it is used as a kind of jigsaw veneer on a metal, stone or marble base. It became a passion in Russia in the first half of the 19th century and the architect Auguste-Richard de Montferraud created a malachite room in the Winter Palace.

(G. Sarti Antiques)

498 A pair of gilded and patinated bronze cassolettes
French, *c*1820
37cm (14½in)
One shown with the lid reversed to reveal the candle nozzle in the form of a flower.

499

500

501

499 A silver-gilt chamber candlestick
Paris, *c*1810
Marc Jacquait
12.2cm (4¾in) wide

500 A porcelain chamber candlestick
English (Worcester), *c*1820–25
Flight, Barr & Barr
10cm (4in) wide
Painted with shells, possibly by Barker

501 A silver chamber candlestick
London, 1789
Hester Bateman; snuffers maker's mark W.B.
9.5cm (3¾in)

502 A silver-gilt snuffers and tray
London, 1808/9
Tray: Paul Storr; snuffers: maker's mark W.B., both for Rundell, Bridge & Rundell
27.3cm (10¾in) wide

502

503 Two designs from a manufacturer's pattern book
English, early 19th century

(Trustees of the Victoria & Albert Museum, London)

504 Catalogue of G.A. Glick
English, early 19th century
Showing alternative designs for a candlestick, with or without support for a storm shade, and with careful instructions as to which sections were patinated and which gilded.

(Trustees of the Victoria & Albert Museum, London)

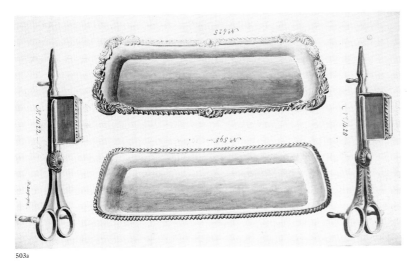

503a

503b

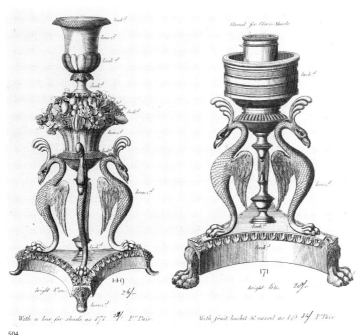

504

505

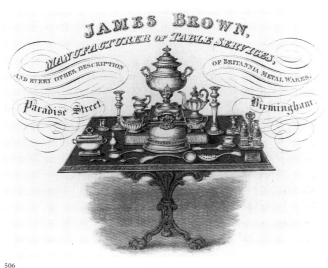

506

505 A patinated and gilded bronze candlestick
English, *c*1810
16.5cm (6½in)
The lead-filled based stamped: Cheney London, published Decr.1809. This candlestick is obviously taken from the design in no.504, though naughty Mr Cheney has not followed the instructions on the gilding exactly.

506 Advertisement from *The History, Topography and Directory of Warwickshire*
English, published 1835
Throughout the 18th century pewterers developed an alloy, first introduced to England by James Taudin in the 17th century, which incorporated antimony. The aim was to produce a harder metal than traditional pewter. In 1769 James Vickers acquired the 'recipe' for Britannia Metal, which omitted lead; it could be rolled into sheet, die stamped, spun or cast. Thus it was possible to produce wares very cheaply, sometimes using the same dies as for the more expensive Sheffield Plate. A new industry developed, based in Sheffield and Birmingham, catering for the lower end of the domestic market. The manufacture of candlesticks was a good proportion of the output.

(Private collection)

507 A silver six-light centrepiece
London, 1822
William Elliott, retailed by
Thomas Hamlet
73.5cm (29in)
Thomas Hamlet included the
Duke of Cambridge among his
clients; however, after an
interesting career he
unfortunately went bankrupt. For
a time he was in partnership with
Francis Lambert (later Lambert
& Rawlings). He and Kensington
Lewis (who was patronized by the
Duke of York) were two of the
more successful rivals to Rundell,
Bridge & Rundell in London in
the early 19th century.

507

508 Design for a centrepiece
English, early 19th century
Attributed to Thomas Stothard
or William Theed
William Theed (1764–1817) was
head of design and chief modeller
at Rundell's, where the sculptor
Thomas Stothard RA was also
employed as a designer between
1809 and 1815.

*(Trustees of the Victoria & Albert
Museum, London)*

509 A silver candelabrum
London, 1816
Paul Storr for Rundell, Bridge &
Rundell
61cm (24in)

510 A silver-gilt centrepiece
London, 1813
Paul Storr for Rundell, Bridge &
Rundell
24in (61.2cm)
The design of this centrepiece is
similar to a drawing attributed to
Thomas Stothard or Edward
Hodges Baily (both designers for
Rundell's) in the Victoria &
Albert Museum, London.

*(Now in the Gilbert collection,
Los Angeles)[92]*

[92] Timothy B. Schroder, *The Gilbert
Collection of Gold and Silver*, Los Angeles,
1988, no.104

508

509

510

511

511 A silver centrepiece
London, 1824
Emes and Barnard
86.5cm (34in)
With a presentation inscription to
Sir Edward Barnes, Governor of
Ceylon 1824–31.

The vase is recorded in the
Barnard ledgers as costing
£895.17s.2d. when ordered
through the retailer Fisher,
Braithwaite and Jones. The
design is copied from a vase in
Piranesi's *Vasi, candelabri, cippi
…* (1778). The casting patterns
still survive.[93]

(Hancocks & Co.)

512 A silver candelabrum
London, 1805–7
Benjamin Smith & Digby Scott
for Rundell, Bridge & Rundell
90cm (35½in)
Engraved with the initial S below
a coronet for HRH The Duke of
Sussex.

The candelabra shown here
and in no.513, owned by two of
George IV's brothers, were made
in several versions for Rundell's,
with a variety of detail.[94] The
Duke of Sussex was not as
extravagant as his brother
Frederick, Duke of York, who
patronized Kensington Lewis,
rather than Rundell's. The sale of
the latter's 'Magnificent silver and
silver-gilt' in 1827 included a
large number of candelabra and
candlesticks, several by Auguste,
and more in ormolu.

513 A pair of silver-gilt
candelabra
London, 1804
Digby Scott & Benjamin Smith
for Rundell, Bridge & Rundell
64.5cm (25¼in)
Numbered 1 and 2 and engraved
with scratch weights.

Applied with the arms of Ernest
Augustus, King of Hanover,
Duke of Cumberland
(1771–1851), the fifth son of
George III. Engraved with the
initials E.D.C. (for Ernest Duke
of Cumberland) and E.A.Fs (for
Ernest Augustus Fideikommis,
the entailed estate of Ernest
Augustus).

[93] Timothy B.Schroder, *The Gilbert Collection
of Gold and Silver*, Los Angeles, 1988,
no.121

[94] For example, see also a pair now in the
Dining Room, Brighton Pavilion

512

513

514

515

516

514 A silver candelabrum
London, 1794
John Scofield
22¼in (56.5cm)
Engraved with the monogram of
Harriet, Duchess of St Albans
(1777–1837). In 1815, four days
after the funeral of his first wife
(who had been his brother's
housemaid), the banker, Thomas
Coutts, then aged eighty-three,
married the young Harriet,
having met her in the Green
Room of Drury Lane Theatre: she
was an actress.[95] On his death
Thomas Coutts left her some
£600,000 and in 1827 she
married the 9th Duke of St
Albans (1801–49). When she
died, most of her estate was
inherited by Thomas Coutts'
grand-daughter Angela, later
Baroness Burdett-Coutts.

515 A silver candelabrum
London, 1800
William Pitts
43.8cm (17¼in)
The lyre is not often seen on
candlesticks but can be found on
a design by Jean-Charles
Delafosse.[96]

516 A gilded bronze
candelabrum
English, *c*1800
51cm (20in)
Engraved with the arms of
Cowper for Peter, 5th Earl
Cowper (1778–1837)

517 Design for a candelabrum
Late 18th century
Giuseppe Boschi
Boschi was born *c*1766 and
known to have been working in
Rome in 1783. It is thought he
worked with Henry Holland and
C.H. Tatham in England.
Tatham was sponsored by
Holland on a visit to Rome where
he bought objects and
commissioned designs for his
patron. In a letter dated 10 July
1795 Tatham sent to London
designs by Giuseppe Valadier,
Antonio Righetti and Boschi,
writing 'each of them are
proprietors of an extensive trade
in bronzes'.

*(Trustees of the Victoria & Albert
Museum, London)*

518 Design for a candelabrum
Charles Heathcote Tatham,
dated 1796
C.H. Tatham (1772–1842) was
employed as a draughtsman by
Henry Holland, who helped him
to visit Italy. He arrived in Rome
in May 1794, but had to leave in
1796 as Napoleon's armies
advanced on Rome. Many of his
designs are based on classical
originals which he drew while in
Italy. This design is based on the
Farnese candelabrum.[97]

*(Trustees of the Victoria & Albert
Museum, London)*

517

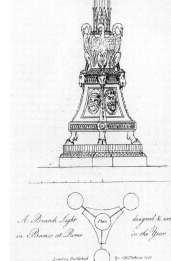

518

[95] Edna Healey, *Lady Unknown*, London,
1978

[96] Museé des Arts Décoratifs, Paris, no.8445

[97] Now in the National Museum in Naples

519

520

521

519 A group of candelabra
French, *c*1825–40
66cm, 47cm and 63.8cm (26in, 18½in and 25in)

520 A silver candelabrum
Paris, *c*1825
Jean-Charles Cahier; stamped: C.Cahier
63.5cm (25in)
Applied with the monogram of Grand Duke Michael Pavlovitch. The Grand Duke's service, executed by Martin-Guillaume Biennais, included over 1,000 pieces. In order to carry out the large orders he received – many from the Russian court – he collaborated with the goldsmith J.-C. Cahier who, on Biennais' retirement in 1819, took over the firm.

521 A gilded bronze candelabrum
English, *c*1825
80cm (31½in)
The stem entwined by a serpent is possibly inspired by the Flaxman drawing no.531.

522

523

522 A silver six-light centrepiece
London, 1803
Philip Cornman for Rundell,
Bridge & Rundell
38cm (15in)
On 29 October 1801 the
Jamaican House of Assembly
passed a resolution to provide
1,000 guineas for the purchase of
a piece of plate to be presented to
the Earl of Balcarres. Alexander
Lindsay, the 6th Earl, was
Lieutenant-Governor of the
island 1794–1801 – hence the
allegorical panels and turtle
supports; his arms, and those of
the island, are applied to the
plinth. Although the designer of
this piece has not been discovered,
Cornman is known to have
followed the designs of J-J.
Boileau and C.H. Tatham.

523 A gilded-bronze
candelabrum
Russian, early 19th century
30.5cm (12in)

524 A gilded bronze
candelabrum
English, c1825
89cm (35in)
The base is engraved with the
arms of James Duff, 4th Earl of
Fife (1776–1857).

525 A porcelain candelabrum
French, c1830
Jacob Petit
82cm (32¼in)

524

525

The human figure became ever more popular as a support for candelabra – often a scantily draped female figure or, as the taste for all things Egyptian escalated, a scantily dressed Nubian or Egyptian slave.

526

527

528

529

526 A gilded and patinated bronze candelabrum
French, *c*1800
119cm (47in)

527 A gilded and patinated bronze candelabrum
French, *c*1825
109cm (43in)

528 A gilded and patinated bronze candelabrum
French, *c*1815

529 A gilded and patinated bronze candelabrum
French, early 19th century
Stamped Chibout
116.5cm (3ft 9¾in)
A family of bronziers bearing the name of Chibout or Chiboust is recorded working in Paris in the second and third quarters of the 18th century. However, there is no documentation for a bronzier of that name working in the Empire period, nor is there a Chibout recorded in the *capitation* of 1786.

530

530 Design showing alternatives
for a chimney-piece and garniture
with two different candelabra
French, late 18th century
Attributed to Pierre-Philippe
Thomire

(Musée des Arts Décoratifs, Paris)

531 Designs for candelabra
John Flaxman, *c*1810

*(Trustees of the Victoria & Albert
Museum, London)*

532 Design for a candelabrum
French, *c*1825
Signed: B. Pecheux

*(Trustees of the Victoria & Albert
Museum, London)*

533 Design for a centrepiece
French, *c*1825
Signed: B. Pecheux

*(Trustees of the Victoria & Albert
Museum, London)*

534 A silver candelabrum
London
Philip Rundell, 1821; the
branches: John Bridge, 1830, for
Rundell, Bridge & Co.
After a design by John Flaxman
110.5cm (3ft 7½in)
The stem represents the apple-
tree in the garden of the
Hesperides with the serpent
Laden being fed by Aegela,
Erytheia and Hesperethusa, the
daughters of Erebus and Night.[98]
The design is based on a drawing
by Flaxman of *c*1809[99] and on
that of no.531.

*(The Worshipful Company of
Goldsmiths, London)*

[98] *John Flaxman, RA*, exh. cat., Royal
Academy of Arts, London, October-
December, 1979, no.185a

[99] op.cit., no.192, in the British Museum

531a   531b

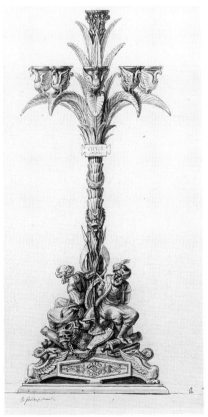

532

533

534

535

535 A blue and white biscuit
clock garniture
Paris (Nast), *c*1800
In imitation of Wedgwood
jasperware, with gilded bronze
mount; the candlesticks formed as
Egyptian water-carriers,

536 A gilded and patinated
bronze clock garniture
French, *c*1820
Candelabra: 43cm (17in)

537 A pair of gilded and
patinated bronze and griotte
marble candelabra
French, early 19th century
82cm (32½in)

536

538 Design for a candelabrum in
bronze
French school, early 19th century
The figural support is in Egyptian
style. After Napoleon's Nile
campaign and the publication of
Baron Vivant Denon's drawings
of Egyptian architecture and
antiquities, there was a great
interest and fashion for objects in
the 'goût d'Egypte'.

*(Trustees of the Victoria & Albert
Museum, London)*

537

538

539

539 Figures in an interior
Italian, early 19th century
Attributed to Raphael Mattioli
The pair of candelabra may well
be of Italian manufacture,
imitating contemporary French
models similar to those shown in
nos 528 and 529.

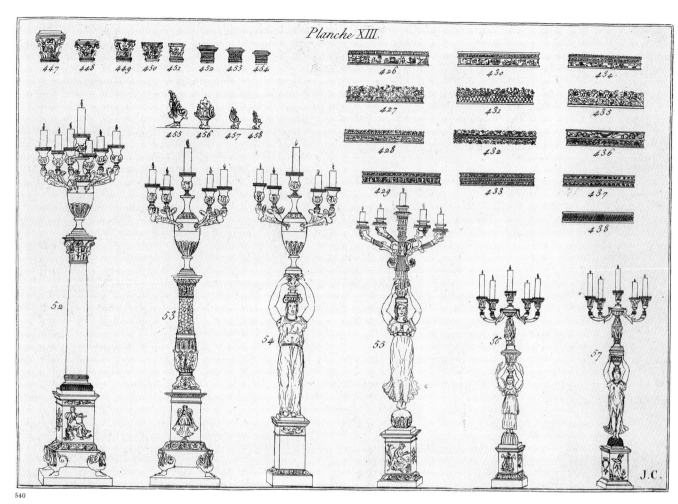

540

540 Plate from the trade catalogue of Mons. Chopin of 257 rue St Denis, Paris, early 19th century
Maker of a wide range of lighting and other metal goods.

(Trustees of the Victoria & Albert Museum, London)

541

542

541 Design for a figural candelabrum
French, *c*1815

(Trustees of the Victoria & Albert Museum, London)

542 Design for a candelabrum
Jean-Guillaume Moitte (1746–1810)
In 1810 the silversmith Jean-Baptiste-Claude Odiot purchased the stock of designs of Henri Auguste after his bankruptcy. These included work by Moitte as well as Charles Percier, Robert-Joseph Auguste and Henri Auguste.

543 A bronze, gilded bronze and marble candelabrum
English, *c*1805
Probably by George Bullock
69cm (27¼in)
An almost identical pair of candelabra at Broughton Hall in Yorkshire was supplied by George Bullock in 1805. In the accompanying bill the bronze figures are described as being French, the implication being that Bullock imported the figures from France and added the candle-arms and bases in England.

544 A silver candelabrum
London, 1815
Paul Storr for Rundell, Bridge & Rundell
43cm (18in)

543

544

545 A pair of cut-glass and gilded plaster candelabra, on white marble bases
English, dated 1809
25.5cm (10in)
Each bears a slightly different inscription on the back: one is inscribed 'publish as the act direct by J.D. Gonelli August 24 1809', the other 'publish as the act Direct July the 14 1809 by J.D. Gonelli'.

545

546 General Norcliffe Norcliffe
in his study at Langton Hall
(detail)
English, *c*1840
Many of the furnishings date
from the early 19th century,
including the pair of figural
candelabra on the chimney-piece
and the little elephant candlestick
on the table (perhaps produced
by the Weeks Museum).

547 Design for the decoration of
the wall of a room, French school,
*c*1780. The chimney-pieces with
figural candelabra of almost
Empire form, the candle-holders
being in the shape of classical
lamps.

(Houtakker collection)

546

547

548 A gilded bronze, tôle and
glass chandelier
French, *c*1819
Claude Galle
110cm (43½in)
The inspiration for this piece
must stem from the series of
much-publicized balloon ascents
of the late 18th and early 19th
centuries, commencing with the
Montgolfiers' in 1783.

The 'fondeur-doreur' Claude
Galle worked for both Louis XVI
and Napoleon and at the time of
Louis XVIII's restoration to the
throne of France, Galle offered to
the Garde Meuble de la
Couronne pieces that he had
made for the various Paris
Exhibitions. Among these objects
figures the following description
of a piece made for the *Exposition
des Produits de l'Industrie
Française* in 1819.

'Lustre à Poisson, au milieu
d'un globe émaillé en bleu et
parsemé d'étoiles est un cercle
avec les signes du zodiaque et six
griffons portant des lumières. De
six patères placés entre chaque
griffon partent douze branches
ornées de ciselure; des ornements
de bon goût en arabesque
supportent l'anneau destiné à
prendre le lustre; au dessous du
cercle sur lequel sont placées les
lumières six branches légères
ornées d'enroulements
suspendent une cuvette en cristal
garnie d'une rich galerie et qui se
termine par un culot dans lequel
est placé san être vu un bouchon
destiné à renouveller l'eau que
l'on place dans la cuvette avec les
petits poissons rouges dont le
mouvement continu récrée l'oeil
agéablement. hauter du lustre 4.
Pieds, diamètre 2. Pieds IIPo. ce
lustre à été exposé . . . 3000 2400
(livres).'

Two almost identical
chandeliers exist;[100] both are
hung with festoons of glass drops,
lacking in the present example.

[100] One in the Swedish Royal Collection,
acquired by King Karl IV Johan sometime
after 1810; the second in the J. Paul Getty
Museum, Malibu

548

549

550

549 A gilded bronze, porcelain and cut-glass chandelier
French, *c*1810
76cm (30in)
The porcelain bowl is decorated to simulate porphyry and bears the mark of the Sarreguemines factory, which was founded in 1784. In 1806 it first exhibited pieces made in imitation of porphyry and in 1810 delivered a set of garden vases in this ware for Napoleon. In the Musée Marmottan in Paris there exists a pair of torchères in porphyry ware with gilded bronze mounts by de la Fontaine, made for the Empress Josephine.[101] It is possible that de la Fontaine was attached to the Sarreguemines factory and also made the mounts for the illustrated chandelier.

550 A gilded wood chandelier
Italian, *c*1830
122cm (4ft 2in)

[101] Another pair was in the collection of the Grand Duke Nicholas Mikhailovitch, and a third pair is in the Throne Room in the Royal Palace in Naples.

551 Design for a chandelier
French, early 19th century
Bound in a volume with other
designs for Morant & Co., 91
New Bond Street, London

An annotation to the design
informs us that the chandelier
would have cost £23 gilded and
£19 plain.

*(Trustees of the Victoria & Albert
Museum, London)*

552 Design for a chandelier
French school, *c*1820

(Houthakker collection)

553 Plate from the trade
catalogue of Mons. Chopin of
257 rue St Denis, Paris
Early 19th century

*(Trustees of the Victoria & Albert
Museum, London)*

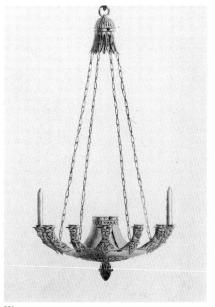

551

552

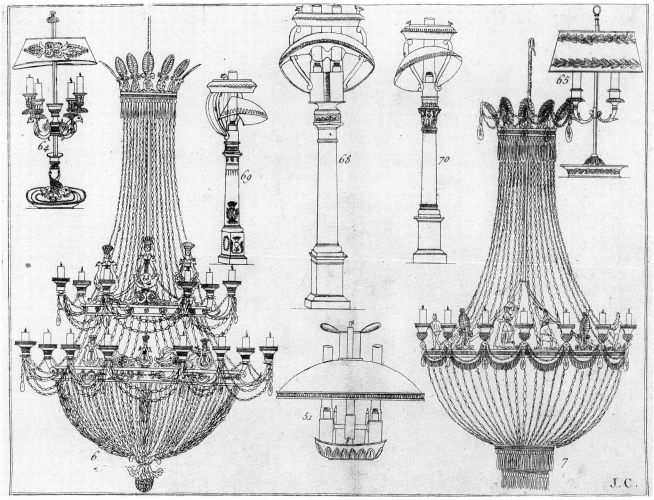

553

554

555

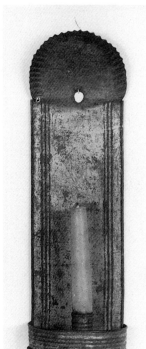

556

557

554 A tin and glass wall-sconce
American, early 19th century
24cm (9½in) diam

(The American Museum in Britain, Bath)

555 A tin wall-light with reflector
American, early 19th century

(Collection Mr J.W. Blum)

556 A tin wall-light
American, 19th century

(Collection Mr J.W. Blum)

557 A painted tin chandelier
American, 19th century
Made to try and imitate glass chandeliers of the type shown in nos 553 and 559.

(Collection Mr J.W. Blum)

558 A blue drawing room
German or Austrian, *c*1840
Showing a chandelier of the same
basic form as that in the following
illustration.

559 A gilded bronze and cut-
glass chandelier
French, *c*1815
92cm (36in)

558

559

560

561

562

560 A silver-gilt library lamp
Paris, 1809–1819, the shade later
Martin-Guillaume Biennais; after
a design by Percier and Fontaine
87.6cm (34½in)
Bearing the arms of Maria Letizia
Ramolino Bonaparte, mother of
Emperor Napoleon, who became
known as Madame Mère, after
being declared by Imperial
proclamation in 1805 'Son
Altesse Impériale, Madame Mère
de l'Empereur'. A year later
J-B-C. Odiot completed a large
service for her.[102]

The firms of Biennais and
Odiot were the finest silversmiths
in Paris in the early 19th century:
between them they supplied the
majority of plate commissioned
by Napoleon, who allocated
100,000 francs a year for silver.
This was increased to 500,000
francs after 1811, not including
special commissions. On his
retirement in 1819, Biennais'
business was continued by J-C.
Cahier (see no.520).

[102] Pieces from the Madame Mère service
were sold at Sotheby's, New York, 28
October 1987

561 A gilded bronze and
mother-of-pearl candlestick with
shade
Vienna, c1825
28.5cm (11¼in)
The painted shade, adjustable in
height according to the level of
the candle, is by Christoph
Mahlknecht (1787–1851) and
shows a view of the Spinnerin am
Kreuz with Vienna in the
background.

562 A gilded bronze, mother-of-
pearl and granite candelabrum
with shade
Vienna, c1820
The delicately painted flowers on
the shade would give a charming
effect with the candle-light
behind in an interior like that
shown in no.303.

563 An ivory and burr ash
candlestick with folding shade
Vienna, c1820
35.5cm (14in)

563

564 La Bouillotte
French, *c*1800
The avid players sit around a
bouillotte table lit by a gilded
bronze bouillotte lamp. On the
chimney-piece stand a pair of
candlesticks and above it hang a
pair of oil lights, probably in tôle.

(Private collection)

565 A gilded bronze bouillotte
lamp
French, *c*1900
69cm (27½in)
This is a late copy of an early
19th-century lamp.

564

565

566a

566

567

568

566 A sheet-iron and brass lamp
Philadelphia, 1849–59
Ellis H. Archer & Redwood F.
Warner
58.5cm (23in)
On marble base, the brass with
matt and burnished patination to
simulate gilding.
    The firm of Archer & Warner
was well known for supplying
girandoles and gas-lighting
appliances. The candle-holding
cylinders are fitted with springs
which push the candles up to the
same constant height as they burn
down. Both these and the shade
are adjustable in height.

(Private collection)

567 A candle screen
American, first half 19th century
Decorated with watercolour
drawings

(The American Museum in Britain, Bath)

569

568 Plate from a manufacturer's catalogue of
'lustres and candelabra'
English, early 19th century
Showing 'Bronz Candle Lamps Engrav'd half
size' and with a similar spring mechanism to
no.566.

(Trustees of the Victoria & Albert Museum, London)

569 Advertisement from *The History,
Topography and Directory of Warwickshire*
English, published 1835
William Mole, 21 Paradise Street,
Birmingham; advertising 'watch & taper
stand, candlesticks & in Bronze & Ormolu'.

(Private collection)

169

570 A pair of cut-glass and gilded bronze candelabra
English, c1810
81cm (32in)
These candelabra are attributed to the firm of Blades, who had a showroom in St Paul's Churchyard, London. The design for a similar pair, made for the King of Persia, is in the Victoria & Albert Museum.

(Jeremy Ltd)

571 A cut-glass and gilded brass candelabrum
English, c1815
44.5cm (17½in)

572 A gilded bronze wall-light
French, c1825
51cm (20in) projection from wall

573 A painted and gilded plaster, cut-glass and gilded metal wall-light
English, c1820

570

571

572

573

574

574 A gilded wood girandole glass
English, *c*1810
The frame in the form of entwined snakes.

575 Portrait of a girl in an interior
American, *c*1825
With a girandole glass similar to that in no.574.

575

In 1809 the sinumbra (without shadow) lamp was patented to overcome the difficulty of the shadow cast by the reservoir of the Argand lamp. Here the oil is contained in a hollow ring which also acts as a support for the shade. The oil is fed from the ring down tubes, which are also supports for the ring, to the burner slightly below and at the centre of the ring.

576

Glasses are   *charged Separately*

577

576 A gilded metal sinumbra lamp
French, *c*1825
68.5cm (27in)

577 A plate from a catalogue showing lamps
English, *c*1825

(Trustees of the Victoria & Albert Museum, London)

578 Pencil sketch of a drawing room
Caroline Elizabeth Hamilton, Woodstock, Oxfordshire, dated 1830
The room is lit by what would appear to be two sinumbra lamps.

(Museum of English Rural Life, Reading)

578

In choosing the source of our light, the great points to be considered are, first the influence on the eyes, and secondly, economy. It is poor economy to use a bad light.

The effect produced by light on the eyes depends upon the following points: First, *Steadiness*. Nothing is more injurious to the eyes than a flickering, unsteady flame ... Second, *Color*. This depends greatly upon the temperature of the flame. A hot flame gives a bright, white light; a flame which has not a high temperature gives a dull, yellow light, which is very injurious to the eyes. In the naked gas-jet a large portion of the flame burns at a low temperature, and the same is the case with the flame of the kerosene lamp when the height of the chimney is not properly proportioned to the amount of oil consumed; a high wick needs a high chimney. In the case of a well-trimmed Argand oil lamp, or an Argand burner for gas, the flame is in general most intensely hot, and the light is of a clear white character. ...

C.C. BEECHER AND HARRIET BEECHER STOWE: *The American Woman's Home or, Principles of Domestic Science*, 1869, quoted by Major L.B.Wyant, 'The Etiquette of Nineteenth-Century Lamps', *Antiques*, September 1936

The best lamp oil is that which is clear and nearly colourless, like water. None but the winter-strained oil should be used in cold weather. Thick, dark-coloured oil burns badly (particularly if it is old) and there is no economy in trying to use it. Unless you require a great deal every night, it is well not to get more than two or three gallons at a time, as it spoils by keeping. Oil that has been kept several months will frequently not burn at all.

Miss Leslie's Housebook, Philadelphia, 1840, quoted by Major L.B.Wyant, 'The Etiquette of Nineteenth-Century Lamps', *Antiques*, September 1936

In buying astral lamps for the table, choose the shades of plain ground glass as they give the clearest and steadiest light and are best for the eyes ... Lamp shades painted in bright colours are now considered in very bad taste ... The fashion of having shades decorated with flowers or other devises, cut on the glass and left transparent is also on the decline ... though it may do well for mantel lamps and lustres.

Miss Leslie's Housebook, Philadelphia, 1840, quoted by Major L.B.Wyant, 'The Etiquette of Nineteenth-Century Lamps', *Antiques*, September 1936

579 Pumping oil before an oil shop
George Scharf (1788–1860)

(Trustees of the British Museum, London)

579

580

580 Mr Oliver's room at
Peterhouse, Cambridge
Watercolour drawn by him in
1830 when he was a Fellow. On
the small table on the right is a
sinumbra lamp.

(Private collection)

581 The Drawing Room,
Rempstone Hall,
Nottinghamshire, 1838
Reuben Turner
With a hanging sinumbra lamp.

582 A gilded and patinated
bronze sinumbra lamp with
opaline glass shade
Probably Low Countries, *c*1830
81cm (32in)

581

582

583

583 A colza oil hanging light
*c*1825
129.5cm (4ft 3in)
Very similar in feeling to the design of no.585
and probably originally fitted with sinumbra
rings and oil burners. The firm of Thomas
Messenger of Birmingham produced very
similar grand hanging oil lights to the
illustrated example, and this may well be from
this firm.

(Phillips)

584 A gilded bronze chandelier
English, 2nd quarter 19th century

585 Design for a hanging oil light with
sinumbra lamps
English, *c*1830
Perry & Co.

(Trustees of the Victoria & Albert Museum, London)

584

585

586

586 The gallery at Apsley House,
designed for the Duke of
Wellington, 1827–8

This view shows the gallery set up
for a banquet and interestingly
the table is arranged around a pair
of floor-standing lights in marble
and gilt-bronze, which are still in
the house.

*(Trustees of the Victoria & Albert
Museum, London)*

On the management of Astral Lamps
The lamp-scissors should be very sharp, or it will be
impossible to trim the wick properly. When you light the
lamp remove the shade and the chimney, and ignite the
wick with a paper match, a supply of which should always
be kept in some convenient place . . . When you wish to
extinguish the lamp entirely turn the screw to the left as far
as it will go . . . When all your lamps have been in use for
company they should next morning be emptied
completely of oil and wick and washed with luke-warm
pearl-ash and water . . . The oil that is removed from these
lamps should be put into a can and saved for use in the
kitchen. On the day of your next company, (and not till
then) replenish them anew. Unless a lamp is used nightly,
no oil and wick should be left in it, even for a single day.

Miss Leslie's Housebook, Philadelphia, 1840, quoted by Major
L.B.Wyant, 'The Etiquette of Nineteenth-Century Lamps',
Antiques, September 1936

587

588

587 A cut-glass chandelier, with
twenty-four lights
English, *c*1830
Perry & Co.
The firm of Perry & Co. was
founded by William Parker in
1756 (see nos 317 and 447), later
it became Parker & Perry, then in
1817 Perry & Co. until its closure
in 1935. They supplied many of
the fittings for Carlton House
and the Royal Pavilion, Brighton.
William Beckford (see
nos.597–600) was also a client.

(Partridge Fine Art)

588 A seven-light wall light with
silvered back plate
English, *c*1820
Perry & Co.
87.5cm (34½in)
This is one of a pair which came
from Hyning Hall, Lancs, home
of Sir Robert Peel, who as
Secretary of State for the Home
Office was responsible for
founding the police force. He
married Julia Floyd in 1820.

(Partridge Fine Art)

589

For four years after his accession in 1820, King George IV did not use Windsor Castle, preferring the more intimate surroundings of Royal Lodge in the park. The castle was gloomy and old-fashioned, little work had been done since the drastic remodelling of the Upper Ward and the Royal Apartments by Hugh May for King Charles II in the 1670s. As well as being inconvenient, these were also in a bad state of repair.

In 1823 eight commissioners were appointed by Parliament to deal with the restoration of the castle, and John Nash, Jeffry Wyatt, Robert Smirke and John Soane were all invited to submit designs for the refurbishment. Soane refused and Wyatt's designs were found preferable to those of Nash and Smirke. Work began in 1824 and it was on the occasion of the laying of the foundation stone that Wyatt asked the King if he might change his name to Wyatville. 'Veal or mutton, call yourself what you like!' was the King's rejoinder.

Work was still going on when the King died in 1830 and was continued under William IV, despite the over-run in costs. The total bill was over £1,000,000 (of which a quarter was for furnishing) against an original grant of £300,000. Wyatville was in charge of the work, but Morel and Seddon were responsible for all the furnishings of the castle and after the demolition of Carlton House in 1837 many pieces were moved from there to Windsor.

The lighting fixtures in the designs illustrated here seem to be all for candle-light and judging from Pine's views of *Royal Residences* published in 1819, it would seem that magnificent oil lamps were to be found at Buckingham House, Kensington Palace and Carlton House, but only in entrance halls and staircases. The formal rooms continued to be lit by candles until almost the end of the nineteenth century.

There was perhaps a feeling that the new form of lighting was bad for the eyes and indeed Madame de Genlis in her *Dictionnaire des Etiquettes* even ascribes the increase in nervous disabilities and the need for spectacles among the young to the replacement of candles by lamps.

589 The circular room at Carlton House
Used at different times as a dining room, music room and reception room, it contained chandeliers possibly by Perry & Co. There were smaller chandeliers in the door bays.

(Private collection)

590 Design for the east wall of the Great Drawing Room, Windsor Castle
Now known as the Crimson Drawing Room, showing the large floor-standing candelabra in gilded bronze which seemed to be George IV's favourite form of lighting. No chandelier is in evidence – unusual in a room of this scale and grandeur.

591 A pair of gilded bronze floor-standing candelabra
French, *c*1815
143.5cm (4ft 8½in)
Of a similar type and style to those shown in the designs for Windsor Castle in nos 590 and 592.

592 Design for the decoration of the north wall of the Great Drawing Room, Windsor Castle

590

591

592

593 A pair of painted and gilded pine candelabra
Danish, *c*1830
Designed by G.F. Hetsch
The design for this pair of candelabra is preserved at the State Archives, Copenhagen. Gustav Friedrich Hetsch (1788–1864) was one of the most notable late Neo-classical designers working in Denmark in the first half of the 19th century. Born in Stuttgart, he studied in Paris, and the influence of his teacher, Charles Percier, pervades his work in the French Empire idiom.

(Carlton Hobbs Ltd)

594 A pair of painted and gilded wood torchères
Italian, early 19th century
311cm (10ft 2in)

595 A pair of brass-inlaid rosewood torchères, with gilded bronze mounts
English, *c*1815
Attributed to George Bullock
198cm (6ft 6in)
These torchères are close to a design in the Wilkinson tracings, a collection of designs from Bullock's workshops.[103] A very similar design also survives in the Trotter albums,[104] though showing the torchères with light fittings. Apart from a slight discrepancy in height (3in, 7.5cm) they closely follow the description of a pair of torchères in Bullock's stock sale:[105]

Lot 63 'A candelabrum of rose-wood, of very sumptuous Buhl manufacture, the upper part of the shaft very splendidly inlaid with brass and mounted with massive or-moulu, the lower part in compartments inlaid with brass, with arabesques of very elegant and tasteful designs, also mounted with masks and ornaments of or-moulu, 6ft 9in high' (£26 to Sir W. Cumming)

Lot 74 was an identical candelabrum, and Lot 75 was a pair of bronze patent lamps, probably intended to sit on top of the pair of candelabra.

(Now in the Walker Art Gallery, Liverpool – Phillips)

596 A carved and gilded wood torchère
French, *c*1815
112cm (3ft 8in)

[103] Now in the Birmingham City Museum and Art Gallery

[104] Recently acquired by the National Monuments Record of Scotland

[105] Christie's, London, 3–5 May 1819, lots 73–74

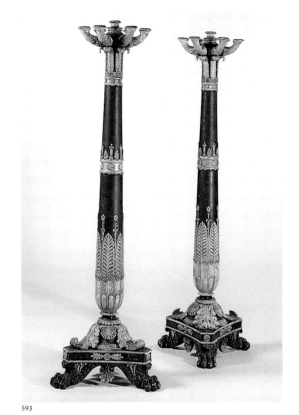

593

594

595

596

597

The taste for Neo-classicism continued well into the nineteenth century, but concurrently an interest was growing in other styles. William Beckford already at the end of the eighteenth century had been passionate about, among other things, the Gothic style, and also bought French furniture. George IV as Prince of Wales had also been greatly influenced by French taste in the furnishings of Carlton House, for which he bought many pieces in France. In the early nineteenth century he elaborated his Pavilion at Brighton in the chinoiserie style. Meanwhile the duchesse de Berry and the comtesse de Boigne (who had visited the Pavilion at Brighton, and found it very sumptuous and agreeable) both showed great enthusiasm for the Gothic Revival taste, as did the comtesse d'Osmonde, all of whom had tremendous influence on contemporary Parisian taste. By the second quarter of the nineteenth century the Rococo revival was in full swing and soon designers were tumbling over each other to find new historicist styles – Islamic, Renaissance, Louis XVI, Mediaeval, Baroque, all followed fairly rapidly.

597 A pair of silver-gilt and gilded bronze candelabra
Paris, 1798–1809
Henri Auguste
52.5cm (20½in)
The silver-gilt bases and gilded bronze branches are cast and applied with cinquefoils and crosses flory, heraldic motifs referring to Beckford's ancestry. Several other pieces made for him have similar decoration, including wall-sconces of 1818 and a lamp for the Oratory at Fonthill.[106] Published views of the interior of Fonthill Abbey include numerous candlesticks.

Beckford also owned a pair of ewers and basins by Henri Auguste, 1787, after designs by Jean Guillaume Moitte.[107] Although the basic form of these candelabra is typical of early 19th-century French models, the decorative detail is in the mediaeval style.

598 A porcelain spill vase
English (probably Ridgway), early 19th century
12.9cm (5in)
Depicting Fonthill Abbey.

598

599

600

599 A silver candlestick
London, 1844
E.E.J. and W. Barnard, designed by Edward English of Bath and modelled by James Short of Bristol (signed: English Bath delt. and Short Bristol Sculpt)
32cm (12½in)
After Beckford sold Fonthill Abbey and most of its contents he moved to Lansdown Crescent, Bath. This candlestick was made for him but probably never delivered, as he died in May 1844. Short's signature appears on a pair of sconces, also by Barnard & Co., dated 1842, made for Beckford.

(Private collection)[108]

600 A silver-gilt candlestick
London, 1800
Paul Storr
Inscribed: Made for the Abbey at Fonthill by Vulliamy & Son, 1800
17.8cm (7in),
These are early examples of silver made for William Beckford in imitation of earlier styles – they follow late 17th-century treen candlesticks, particularly the boxwood carved ware produced by Bagard at Nancy, but were described by Beckford as 'from an original design of Holbein'. Vulliamy's accounts list them as follows: '. . . the whole Gilt and

finished in so perfect a manner as exactly to resemble a pair of highly finished Gold Chased Candlesticks'.[109]

Beckford and his architect, Wyatt, began the building of Fonthill Abbey in the latter part of the 18th century and Beckford continued through several scandals and disasters (the tower fell down twice) until he was forced to sell the estate in 1823.

[106] Michael Snodin and Malcolm Baker, 'William Beckford's Silver I', *Burlington Magazine,* November 1980, figs 18 and 20

[107] Sotheby's, New York, 8 April 1986, lot 72 and Monaco, 24 June 1986, lot 1601

[108] Previously Christie's, New York, 29 April 1987, lot 262

[109] Michael Snodin and Malcolm Baker, 'William Beckford's Silver I', *Burlington Magazine,* November 1980

601

ra for the dining Room

602

602a

601 Design for standing candelabra and lamps
Sir Jeffry Wyatville, *c*1810
(Trustees of the Victoria & Albert Museum, London)

602 A Coade Stone candelabrum or torchère
English, *c*1810
Designed by Thomas Hopper (1776–1856) and made by Coade & Sealy for the Prince of Wales' conservatory at Carlton House
206cm (6ft 9in)
The torchère is one of ten made for the cast-iron and glass conservatory at Carlton House, built by George, Prince of Wales (later Prince Regent and King George IV). Thomas Hopper designed the conservatory in 1807 to celebrate the Welsh title of the Prince, and loosely based the decoration on the chapel of Henry VII at Westminster Abbey.

The centrepiece of the conservatory was a fountain crowned with a bunch of leeks (emblem of Wales), which, with the ten torchères, was cast by Coade and Sealy, the celebrated manufacturers of artificial stone. They charged £50 for each torchère and £97.1s. for the fountain. After the demolition of Carlton House eight of the torchères were gilded, at a cost of £200, by Morel and Seddon and incorporated into Sir Jeffry Wyatville's scheme for the Coffee Room at Windsor Castle (see no.605). The illustrated torchère must be one of these eight, as small traces of gesso and gold-leaf remain in the crevices.

Eleanor Coade's business was at Narrow Wall, Lambeth from 1769 to 1821 and it produced an artificial stone which very successfully imitated natural limestone and was also weatherproof. The pieces had varying stamps during the firm's output and she took as partners two relatives: John Sealy (1799–1813) and William Croggan (1813–21). The latter bought the business on her death and continued it until it went bankrupt in 1833.

(Now in the National Museum of Wales, Cardiff – Christie's)

603 Design for a Gothic-style chandelier, perhaps for Carlton House
Possibly supplied by Parker & Perry in 1814 when J. Nash and T. Hopper were carrying out additions in the Gothic style to Carlton House, though it is more similar in feeling to the chandeliers designed by William Porden between 1803 and 1825 for Earl Grosvenor's vast Gothic mansion at Eaton in Cheshire.

(Trustees of the Victoria & Albert Museum, London)

604 View of the drawing room at Eaton Hall
J. Buckler, from 'Views of Eaton Hall' publ.1826
Showing the house as gothicised by William Porden before the Waterhouse additions. The majority of the house was demolished in the 1960s.

603

604

05

606

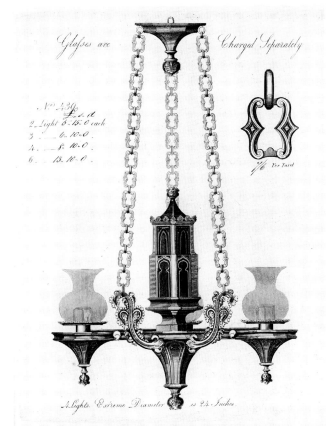

607

608

605 Design for the north wall (?) of the Coffee Room, Windsor Castle (see no.602) Sir Jeffry Wyatville

606 A Gothic Revival gilded bronze candlestick French, *c*1815 32cm (12½in)

(Private collection)

607 Plate from a manufacturer's catalogue English, *c*1825 Showing a hanging oil-light in Gothic style.
The chain was supplied at 7/6d per Yard; the design could be ordered in various sizes, from two lights to six lights.

(Trustees of the Victoria & Albert Museum, London)

608 A silver candlestick London, 1814 William Elliott 28.5cm (11¼in)

609 A gilded brass lantern in the Gothic style
English, *c*1815
Designed by George Bullock
The lantern hung in New Longwood House, the Emperor Napoleon's quarters in exile on St Helena.

Recent research suggests that Bullock did not have the facilities to manufacture large metalwork objects in his own workshop and he is known to have sub-contracted such work to a firm called W.S. Summers in New Bond Street, London.

(Pelham Galleries)

610 A pair of silver candlesticks
London, 1816
Edward Farrell
30cm (11¾in)
From a set of six, the others by John Crouch, 1812. Farrell made a similar design in 1821, engraved with the arms of George IV,[110] and so did Phillips Garden in 1756.

(The Burghley House collection)

611 A gilded bronze candelabrum
English, *c*1820
72.5cm (28½in)

[110]Christie's, London, 24 November, 1971, lot 45

609a

625

625 A silver chandelier for
eighteen lights
London, 1837
Robert Garrard II
152.5cm (60in)
The chandelier, which weighs
2,332oz, was commissioned by
James Hamilton, 2nd Marquess
of Abercorn (1811–85), who
succeeded to the title in 1833 and
was created Duke of Abercorn in
1868. He also bought extensively
from Storr & Mortimer.

(Partridge Fine Art)

626

626 Interior of a drawing room in a town house, *c*1855
Samuel Rayner
The chandelier would appear to be of contemporary Venetian origin. There is a pair of wall-lights on the chimney-piece and a pair of candelabra opposite. By this date, oil lamps would probably have been brought into the room as it became dark.

(Trustees of the Victoria & Albert Museum, London)

627 A large gilded wood and plaster floor-standing candelabrum
English, *c*1840
330cm (10ft 10in)
Made by Thomas Ward of Hull for Sir Thomas Clifford Constable of Burton Constable, Yorkshire, in what was at the time thought to be the Louis XIV style, though it seems more Italianate to our 20th-century eyes.

628 A gilded bronze chandelier
English, *c*1840, in Louis XV style
104cm (41in)

627

628

The Industrial Revolution was slow to affect the craft of the chandler. In the early nineteenth century candles were still made in a way which would have been recognizable to men of two hundred years before and, spermaceti apart, the raw materials of candle-making had not changed in two thousand years.

In 1813 a French chemist, Michel Eugène Chevreul, discovered that if the glycerine content was removed from tallow, the candle burned with a much brighter flame. He tried to market these new candles, made of what he described as 'Stearine', named after the stearic acid in the purified tallow. The use of potash in the purifying process made the production too expensive and it was another Frenchman, de Milly, who substituted lime for potash and produced what he named 'bougies de l'étoile'. These candles were still expensive, but research continued apace and in the 1830s E.Price & Co., tallow merchants, produced a palmatine candle, invented by Dr John Hemple and Henry Blundell, made from coconut palm oil. In 1840 Price & Co. produced a new snuffless candle to co-incide with Queen Victoria's wedding, made from a combination of coconut oil and stearine. They sold for a shilling a pound – cheap enough to become universally popular. In 1820 Cambacères in France had invented the plaited wick, which curled over and burnt away in the edge of the candle flame. Price fitted these to their new candles, thus making them snuffless.

In the second quarter of the nineteenth century paraffin wax was discovered and by the 1850s was used to make candles which burned as brightly as the best beeswax or spermaceti candles. By the end of the nineteenth century most candles were made of paraffin wax. In 1831 the excise duties in Britain on candles and candle-makers were repealed and this also led to expansion. By 1851 Price's employed over nine hundred men in their two factories in Vauxhall and Battersea.

The candle-moulding machines had also advanced with the introduction of the continuous wick in 1796 and the water-jacket in 1801, which could be either hot, to keep the wax molten, or cold to speed up the hardening time.

629 Dipping candles
Illustration from *Cyclopaedia of Useful Arts*, published in London in 1854

(Museum of English Rural Life, Reading)

630 Making nightlights
Illustration from *Cyclopaedia of Useful Arts*, published in London in 1854

(Museum of English Rural Life, Reading)

629

630

631

632

633

631 A pair of porcelain and gilded bronze
candelabra
Dresden, mid-19th century
91cm (36in)
The metal branches are probably later
replacements for porcelain branches which
were broken.

632 A gilded bronze and porcelain
candelabrum
French, *c*1835
87cm (34½in)

633 A porcelain and gilded bronze
candelabrum
The porcelain: Imari, late 17th century; the
mounts: French, mid-19th century, in Louis
XV style
80.5cm (31¾in)

634

635

636

634 A writing desk
French, mid-19th century, in Louis XV style
With candle-branches fitted to the sides.

635 A gilded and patinated bronze and marble candelabrum
Paris, 19th century
After the celebrated model attributed to Pierre-Philippe Thomire
89cm (35in)
The original candelabrum on which the present one is based is known as the 'Candelabre de l'Indépendance Américaine' and is now in the Louvre. It originally stood on a commode by the royal ébéniste Jean-Henri Riesener, in Louis XVI's cabinet-intérieur or private study at Versailles.

The attribution to Thomire rests on his purchase on 12 October 1784 from the Sèvres factory of a 'grand triangle beau bleu' and three 'bas reliéfs bleu et blanc'. Those correspond exactly to the porcelain panels which form the base of the Louvre candelabrum and which are replaced by gilded bronze plaques in the present examples. Interestingly the original candelabrum is recorded as being surmounted by an 'indien tenant de la main droit un arc et de l'autre une massue'. This was replaced in about 1800 by a single candle-holder. The Indian figures which surmount the present candelabra must presumably have been adapted from the original. The native figures represent America, the cockerels France, and the lions with chains in their mouths (lacking in the present examples) the recently defeated England. Thomire is recorded as having made other versions of this model, including examples for Lafayette and Washington.

636 A pair of gilded and patinated bronze candelabra
French, *c*1850
78cm (30¾in)
Showing the Four Seasons.

637

He was walking up and down the dining-room, wishing
that his mother would order candles, and allow him to set
to work at either reading or writing, and so put a stop to
the conversation. But he never thought of interfering in
any of the small domestic regulations that Mrs Thornton
observed, in habitual remembrance of her old economies.

MRS GASKELL, *North and South*, 1854

638

639

640

641

637 A candelabrum from the
Royal Dresden Manufactory,
Meissen
Detail of an illustration taken
from: J.B.Waring, *Masterpieces of
Industrial Art and Sculpture at
the International Exhibition,
1862*, plate 202
    The candelabrum is very similar
in design to those in no.631.

638 A silver taperstick
Birmingham, 1838
Robinson, Edkins & Aston of the
Soho Plate Company
10.2cm (4in) wide

639 A porcelain candlestick
group
English (Minton), *c*1835–40
23.5cm (9¼in)
Showing a gardener and his
companion.

640 A Sheffield Plate chamber
candlestick
English, *c*1850
Mappin Brothers of Sheffield
12.2cm (4¾in) diam

641 Two electroplated chamber
candlesticks, with gimbal handles
English, *c*1848
Elkington, Mason & Co.
15.2cm (6in) and 14.3cm (5¾in)
diam
Each struck with date number for
1848 and applied with a plate:
IBGF'S Patent.

642 Concert Hall in the Castle of
Sagan
E. Hackert, *c*1850
A room lit entirely by candles –
and many of them: two
chandeliers, banks of wall-lights,
torchères in the corners and, most
interesting, rows of candle-
holders over the doorways.

642

I have often noticed that almost every one has his own individual small economies. Now Miss Matty Jenkyns was chary of candles. We had many devices to use as few as possible. In the winter afternoons she would sit knitting for two or three hours – she could do this in the dark, or by firelight – and when I asked if I might not ring for candles to finish stitching my wristbands, she told me to 'keep blind man's holiday'. They were usually brought in with tea; but we only burnt one at a time. As we lived in constant preparation for a friend who might come in any evening (but who never did), it required some contrivance to keep our two candles of the same length, ready to be lighted, and to look as if we burnt two always. The candles took it in turns; and, whatever we might be talking about or doing, Miss Matty's eyes were habitually fixed upon the candle, ready to jump up and extinguish it and to light the other before they had become too uneven in length to be restored to equality in the course of the evening.

MRS GASKELL, *Cranford*, 1853

'We'll put out the candle, my dear. We can talk just as well by firelight, you know.'

MRS GASKELL, *Cranford*, 1853

Many of the Diplomatic Body were in the habit of attending the midnight Mass at St Isaac's on Easter Day, on account of the wonderfully impressive character of the service. . . . As the eye grew accustomed to the shadows, tens of thousands of unlighted candles, outlining the arches, cornices and other architectural features of the cathedral, were just visible. These candles each had their wick touched with kerosene and then surrounded with a thread of gun-cotton, which ran continuously from candle to candle right round the building. When the hanging end of the thread of gun-cotton was lighted, the flame ran swiftly round the church, kindling each candle in turn; a very fascinating sight.

At Tsarskoye Selo (Nicholas Hall):

As electric light had not then been introduced into the palace, the entire building was lighted with wax candles. I cannot remember the number I was told were required on these occasions (Court balls) but I think it was over one hundred thousand. The candles were all lighted with a thread of gun-cotton, as in St Isaac's Cathedral.

LORD FREDERICK HAMILTON, *Vanished Pomps of Yesterday*, 1919

643

643 Page from a pattern book
English, *c*1835
H. and R. Daniel of Stoke
Showing a design for a Rococo
revival candlestick in porcelain,
similar but less elaborate than that
in no.646.

*(Trustees of the Victoria & Albert
Museum, London)*

644 A pair of silver-gilt
candlesticks
London, 1857
Edward Barnard & Sons
16.5cm (6½in)

645 A silver taperstick
London, 1840
Edward Barnard & Sons
10.2cm (4in)

*(Now in the Victoria & Albert
Museum, London)*

646 A porcelain candlestick
English (Minton), *c*1830
23.5cm (9¼in)

644

645

646

The fire was made up; the neat maid-servant had received
her last directions; and there we stood, dressed in our best,
each with a candle-lighter in our hands, ready to dart at the
candles as soon as the first knock came. Parties in Cranford
were solemn festivities . . .

MRS GASKELL, *Cranford*, 1853

Two wax candles stood lighted on the table and two on
the mantelpiece; basking in the light and heat of a superb
fire, lay Pilot – Adèle knelt near him.

CHARLOTTE BRONTË, *Jane Eyre*, 1847

She groped her way to the taper and the lucifer matches.
She suddenly felt shy, when the little feeble light made
them visible. All she could see was that her brother's face
was unusually dark in complexion . . .

MRS GASKELL, *North and South*, 1854

647

647 Watercolour of the drawing room at the château de Ferrières designed by the British architect Paxton, for the French Rothschilds in the mid-19th century

It shows several pairs of candelabra in the Louis XVI style, a large chandelier hung with rock-crystal dating from the mid-18th century, and an enormous pair of Chinese porcelain covered vases, dating from the 18th century but converted into candelabra in the 19th century.

(Private collection)

648

648 A cut-glass chandelier
English, *c*1850
Osler of Birmingham
The firm of S. & C. Osler was a renowned glass manufacturing firm established in 1807 by Thomas Osler; it closed finally in 1976. Ibrahum Pascha visited Birmingham in 1847 and commissioned a pair of chandeliers for the tomb of the prophet Mohammed. This established the firm's reputation and the Prince Consort consolidated their importance by buying a pair of chandeliers for Queen Victoria in 1848, now at Osborne House. The company successfully exhibited at the Great Exhibition in 1851.

(Mallett)

649

650

651

652

653

654

649 The evening drink
Johannes Rosierse

650 A silver candlestick
German, mid-19th century
Stamped: Schott
31cm (12¼in)

651 A canary-yellow sandwich-
glass candlestick
American, mid-19th century
26.8cm (10½in)

652 A silver die-stamped
candlestick
Sheffield, 1845
Henry Wilkinson & Co.
26.5cm.(10½in)

653 A glass candlestick
Varnish & Co., *c*1850
33cm (13in)
The campana-shaped sconce in
silver and red, with a basalt-gilt
mount in the form of leaves, the
base in silver and green.

654 A silver-gilt and champlevé
candlestick
French, *c*1845
Jean Valentin Morel, stamped:
Morel & Cie
24.2cm (9¼in)

He fastened the door, and walked across the hall, and up
the stairs; slowly too: trimming his candle as he went . . .
Half-a-dozen gas lamps out of the street wouldn't have
lighted the entry too well, so you may suppose that it was
pretty dark with Scrooge's dip.

CHARLES DICKENS, *A Christmas Carol*, 1843

In 1847 James Young invented a process to refine paraffin oil, which revolutionized the oil lamp, it being much less viscous than colza oil. The introduction of the flat wick with good aeration was quickly followed in 1865 by the invention by Joseph Hinks of the Duplex burner, which was both reliable and efficient and much increased the luminosity of the flame. In the years 1859–70 about eighty patents a year were taken out for inventions concerning the oil lamp, mostly to do with designs to produce a better draught, eventually vastly improved by the central draught burner.

By the middle of the nineteenth century, even the most modest households possessed several oil lamps. These lamps all had to have constant maintenance – wicks trimming, oil reservoirs re-filling, globes needed washing, brass parts needed polishing. In larger and richer households lamp maintenance was a full-time job for at least one member of staff and there was often a lamp room where he worked during the day, before taking the lamps around to the various rooms and lighting them.

655 A glass overlay lamp base, with gilded metal mounts and with translucent ruby glass
English, mid-19th century
51cm (20¼in)

656 A pair of overlay glass oil lamps
Bohemian, mid-19th century
66cm (26in)
In green glass overlaid in opaque white, on gilt metal and alabaster foot.

657 An enamelled and gilded glass oil lamp
Bohemian, c1840

655

656

657

658 Watercolour of a library
English, mid-19th century
The piano has a large pair of
porcelain oil lamps standing on it
in what would seem a fairly
permanent position.

*(Trustees of the Victoria & Albert
Museum, London)*

658

659

659 The Boudoir, Rempstone
Hall, Nottinghamshire
Sarah Caroline Sitwell
Showing two differing oil lamps
on the chimney-piece.

660

660 Formal dining room at the Castle of Sagan
E. Hackert, *c*1850
The room has candles in the chandelier and candelabra on the buffet; oil lamps on brackets on the wall and an interesting standing torchère with branches for oil lamps.

661 Salon at the Castle of Sagan, as redecorated for the duchesse de Dino, *c*1850
The chandelier is lit by candles, but there are oil lamps on the brackets around the walls.

661

662 Knitting pattern for a cover for a Hadrot lamp
'This cover is intended to protect the lamp from the dust, which greatly injures the bronzing of the Hadrot lamp.' The recommended colours were: 'half-a-dozen skeins of each of seven shades of green wool, and four of scarlet ditto'.

Illustration taken from: *The Illustrated Exhibitor and Magazine of Art*, July 1852

663 An iron and brass solar lamp
Philadelphia, 1849–53
Cornelius & Co.
63.5cm (25in)
With maker's stamp: Cornelius & Co/
Philad/July 24th 1849/Patent/April 1st
1843

(Private collection)

662

HADROT LAMP COVER.

663

664/665

666

667

664 A patinated bronze oil lamp
French, *c*1880
74cm (29in)

665 A gilded and patinated
bronze oil lamp
French, mid-19th century
Bearing the label of Gagneau,
125 R.Lafayette
76cm (30in)
One of a pair of lamps which have
separate stands which would have
remained in position in the room
where the lamps were to be used
even during the day, when the
lamps themselves would probably
have been removed for cleaning
and re-filling.

666 Design for an oil lamp
Mid-19th century, in Renaissance
revival style
Otto Parz

*(Trustees of the Victoria & Albert
Museum, London)*

667 A night timepiece
French, *c*1870

668 Design for an oil lamp
John Thomas
Inscribed: Candelabra pedestals to staircase Somerleyton Hall
The house at Somerleyton had been done over, regardless of expense
and, many felt, good taste, for the great contractor, Sir Morton Peto,
from 1844–51. The designer was John Thomas, a sculptor and
ornamental mason who had worked on the Houses of Parliament, for
which Peto had been the contractor. It is unclear why this design, so
obviously for an oil lamp on a pedestal, is thus inscribed but, as the oil
lamp would have had to lift out of the base to be cleaned and have its
reservoir re-filled, perhaps there were alternative fittings for candle-
branches.

(Trustees of the Victoria & Albert Museum, London)

668

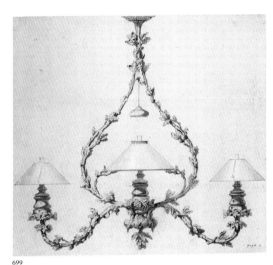

699

669 Design for a hanging oil
light
Paris, mid-19th century
Eugène Vittoz
The oil lamps are all shaded and,
presumably, lift easily off the
frame to be cleaned and re-filled.
Only the central lamp has a
smoke-dome to protect the
metalwork above.

*(Trustees of the Victoria & Albert
Museum, London)*

670 Design for a centrepiece
French, mid-19th century
E. Rambaud
Showing an interesting
alternative for either candelabra
or oil lamps.

(Houthakker collection)

670

205

671 An oil lamp and two vases
London, 1862
Antoine Vechte for Hunt &
Roskell
The damascened lamp was
commissioned by the Marquess of
Breadalbane to incorporate the
Poniatowski collection of
engraved gems. It had interior
lights to show up the gems.

Illustration taken from: J.B. Waring,
*Masterpieces of Industrial Art and
Sculpture at the International
Exhibition, 1862*, plate 202.[117]

**672 Design for a candelabrum
and oil light**
Paris, *c*1860
Eugène Vittoz
Designed to be made using a
Chinese baluster pot at the base,
surmounted by a Chinese beaker
vase, with the cover of the lower
vase just showing above. All
profusely mounted in gilded
bronze, this must have been a
large object, perhaps five or six
feet (150–180cm) tall, and
probably intended to stand on the
floor or on a low plinth. A
somewhat similar pair is shown in
the watercolour of the interior of
the drawing room at Ferrières in
no.647

*(Trustees of the Victoria & Albert
Museum, London)*

673 Design for an oil lamp
Paris, *c*1860
Eugène Vittoz
In Oriental style and, again, using
Chinese porcelain vases in the
design.

*(Trustees of the Victoria & Albert
Museum, London)*

**674 A hanging lamp of Sèvres
porcelain, in Islamic style**

Illustration taken from: M. Digby
Wyatt, *The Industrial Arts of the
Nineteenth Century at the Great
Exhibition, 1851*, plate 115.

[117] For a photograph of the lamp, taken in
1862, see John Culme, *Nineteenth Century
Silver*, London, 1977, p.172

671

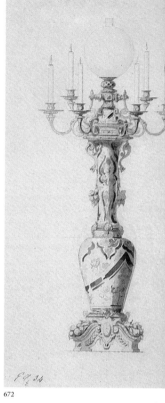

672

673

674

675

The family houses of most of the Austrian nobility were in the Inner Town, the old walled city, where space was very limited. These fine old houses, built for the greater part in the Italian baroque style, though splendid for entertaining, were almost pitch dark and very airless in the daytime … The Lobkowitz Palace, afterwards the French Embassy, was so dark by day that artificial light had always to be used.

LORD FREDERICK HAMILTON, *Vanished Pomps of Yesterday*, 1919

675 Interior of a drawing room
Anon, German, *c*1830
With central hanging oil light.

(Trustees of the Victoria & Albert Museum, London)

676 Interior of a study or morning room
German, *c*1835
With an interesting chandelier which also incorporates an oil lamp.

677 Gunroom at the Castle of Sagan
E. Hackert, *c*1850

676

677

207

678 Four lamps on torchères
By (from left to right): A.
Lacarriere Son & Co.; Raingo
Bros; T. Descole; L. Lerolle

Illustration taken from: J.B.Waring,
*Masterpieces of Industrial Art and
Sculpture at the International
Exhibition, 1862*, plate 257.

679 A pair of parcel-gilt
patinated bronze floor-standing
lamps
French, *c*1880
Each engraved: F. Barbedienne,
Fondeur
150cm (59in)
Formerly for oil, now converted
to electricity.

   In 1830 Barbedienne
(1810–1892) founded one of the
most important French art
foundries. He was renowned for
his masterly reproductions of
French and Italian Renaissance
sculpture. In 1839 he
collaborated with the inventor
Achille Collas who had succeeded
in enlarging and reducing works
of art to arbitrary sizes by a simple
mathematical calculation.
Barbedienne competed with the
production of Japanese and
Chinese enamels, pioneering a
champlevé technique. In 1850 he
was commissioned to furnish the
Paris town hall for which he was
awarded with the 'médaille
d'honneur' at the Paris World
Exhibition in 1855.

680 A small spout lamp, two
candelabra in antique style and a
large vase-shaped oil lamp
F. Gautier of Paris

Illustration taken from: J.B.Waring,
*Masterpieces of Industrial Art and
Sculpture at the International
Exhibition, 1862*, plate 284.

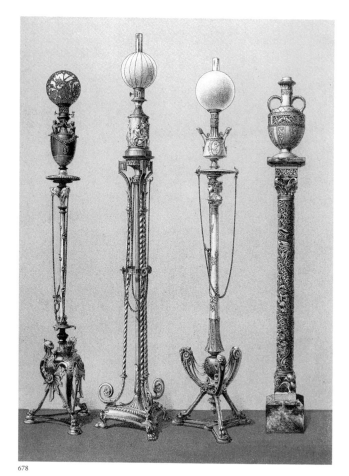

678

679

680

681 A silver centrepiece
London, 1849
E.J. & W. Barnard
84cm (33in)

682 A pair of silver candelabra
London, 1861
T.H. and F. Francis
Retailed by H. Emanuel

(Brand Inglis Ltd)

683 Design for a centrepiece
English, *c*1845

(Trustees of the Victoria & Albert Museum, London)

684 A porcelain clock garniture
Meissen, *c*1860
Candelabra: 36cm (14in)

681

682

683

684

685 A clock garniture in bronze
and black marble
In antique Italian style

Illustration taken from: J.B. Waring,
*Masterpieces of Industrial Art and
Sculpture at the International
Exhibition, 1862*, plate 213.

686 Ludwig II's study in the
Residenz, Munich
Reinhard Sebastian Zimmerman
Ludwig (1845–86) had a passion
for the 18th century and
particularly for the interiors of
Louis XIV. His study appears to
be lit lavishly by candles, which
must have been a conscious
attempt to imitate the previous
century, the more practical oil
lamp having been banished as
being far too modern.

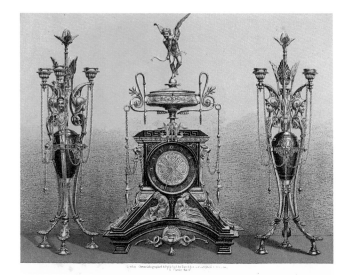

685

686

Her mother made butter, for themselves and to sell, baked their own bread, and made candles for lighting. Not much of a light, Sally said, but it cost next to nothing, and, of course, they went to bed early.

FLORA THOMPSON (1876–1947), *Lark Rise to Candleford*, 1939

Before breakfast at 8 o'clock all the shutters in the main rooms had to be opened, as many as forty oil lamps collected up for adjustment and refilling, and a start made on cleaning grates and laying fires. These jobs were resumed between breakfast and chapel.

MERLIN WATERSON, *The Servants' Hall, a domestic history of Erddig*, London, 1980

The Dowager might be between forty and fifty: her shape was still fine; her hair (by candlelight at least) still black; . . .

CHARLOTTE BRONTË, *Jane Eyre*, 1847

Notwithstanding the generous hospitality of the English country house sixty years ago, the refined luxury which has since become a necessity of entertaining was wanting. The fare was as massive as the plate. After sunset the corridors were dimly lighted by oil lamps, and all that could be seen was the glimmer of armoured figures emerging from the gloom. Passing up the great stairs to bed was a terrifying affair; . . .

VISCOUNT ESHER writing in 1927 about Lowther Castle, seat of the Earl of Lonsdale

687

687 The Vanderbilt family at home
American, *c*1870
Seymour J. Guy
The room, despite the somewhat dour-looking members of the Vanderbilt family, exudes a certain warmth and cosiness thanks to the glow of the many oil lamps on the walls and hanging from the ceiling. The next room, shrouded in darkness, also has an enormous glass hanging oil light. On the chimney-piece are a pair of large candelabra matching a clock, which are roughly contemporary in date to the oil lighting, not a relic of former times, and therefore obviously sometimes used either instead of, or in conjunction with, the oil lighting.

(Biltmore Estate collection)

688 A dinner party at Haddo House, Aberdeenshire
Alfred Edward Emslie, *c*1884
The host and hostess are the Earl and Countess of Aberdeen. Lady Aberdeen is talking to the Prime Minister, Gladstone, and on her left is the 5th Earl of Rosebery, who succeeded Gladstone as Prime Minister and who was the owner of Mentmore Towers (see no.321). The table is lit by shaded candles, while on the chimney-piece is a pair of oil lamps.

(National Portrait Gallery, London)

688

689 An electroplated six-light
candelabrum
English, c1875
71cm (28¼in)

690 Design for a candelabrum
Adrien-Louis Cavelier
(1775–1867)
Inscribed on the verso: Madame
la Bne Gustave de Rothschild de
l'apart de . . .

(Houthakker collection)

691 A silver candelabrum
Paris, c1870
Maison Odiot, stamped: Odiot a
Paris
64.2cm (25¼in)
The stem is based on a celebrated
model of a candlestick in gilded
bronze produced by Martincourt
in the 1780s.

692 Design for a candlestick
Alfred Stevens (1817–75)
Stevens studied in Italy where he
developed an unshakeable passion
for the High Renaissance. His
masterpiece was the interior of
Dorchester House, London
(1858–62).

*(Trustees of the Victoria & Albert
Museum, London)*

693 An electroplate
candelabrum
French, c1870, in 18th-century
taste
Christofle & Cie, Paris
87cm (37¼in)
This is one of a pair engraved with
the arms of the duc de Biron; they
also have order numbers 882741
and 882742.

694 A silver candelabrum
London, 1885
Designed by G.A. Carter for
Hunt & Roskell
Part of a testimonial presented by
the shareholders of the White Star
shipping line to Thomas Henry
Ismay. 'The various pieces have
been designed to illustrate the
Progress of the Art of Navigation
from the Earliest Times to the
Present Day, its Means and
Objects . . . the service . . . has
been three years in the
manufacturers' hands . . . and cost
over four thousand guineas.'[118]

[118] Contemporary descriptions quoted by
John Culme, *Nineteenth Century Silver,*
London, 1977, p.114

689

690

691

692

693

694

695 A burmese glass fairy
pyramid nightlight stand
English, c1887
Thos. Webb & Sons; drip-pans:
Samuel Clarke
The base marked: 'Thos Webb &
Sons Queen's burmeseware
patented' and with 'S Clarke's
Fairy patent trademark'
The first burmese glass
nightlights were introduced in
January 1887 when Samuel
Clarke asked Thomas Webb &

Sons to make shades in their new
process, the trademark of which
they had patented a few months
previously.
Although designed to burn
nightlight candles (see no.630), it
was more likely that this
candelabrum was intended to
stand on a dining-table, with
flowers in the trumpet-shaped
holders.

696 A pair of novelty
candlesticks
London, 1877
William Frederick Williams
17cm (6¾in)
The silver-mounted tusks
forming owls with coloured glass
eyes and wearing top-hats.

(Phillips)

212

695

696

697/698

699

700

701

697 An ivory candlestick
Possibly French, mid-19th
century
22cm (8¾in)

698 A bronze and ivory
candlestick
Mid-19th century
Figure: possibly Chinese; the
mounts: French
24cm (9½in)

699 A porcelain candlestick
English (Minton), late 19th
century
Charles Toft
33.7cm (13¼in)
Charles Toft specialized in
producing 'St Porchaire' wares first
for Minton's in the 1860s and
1870s, and then for Wedgwood.[119]
This is one of a pair of candlesticks
directly based on the St Porchaire
candlestick in the Victoria &
Albert Museum, no.34.

700 A 'majolica' candlestick
English (Minton), late 19th
century
40.8cm (16in)

701 A silver chamber candlestick
Lucerne, *c*1880
Johann Karl Bossard
21.5cm (8½in)

702 A 'majolica' clock garniture
English (Wedgwood), *c*1870

703 A bisque porcelain
candelabrum
German (KPM), 2nd half 19th
century
Signed: R. Möller
46cm (18in)
In predominantly blue and pink
pastel tones.

702

703

[119]Paul Atterbury, 'Too Good to be True',
*Country Life,*14 June 1990

704 A drawing-room in Vienna
Franz Alt (1821–1906)
Dated 1872
With a large chandelier in
mid-18th-century style.

705 A chandelier in Indian style
Matifat of Paris

Illustration taken from: M. Digby
Wyatt, *The Industrial Arts of the
Nineteenth Century at the Great
Exhibition, 1851*, plate 139.

706 A gilded bronze chandelier
French, *c*1875
114cm (45in)
In Louis XV style, directly
copying an 18th-century
model.[120]

[120] Now in the Bibliothèque Mazarin in
Paris.

704

705

706

707 A painted ruby overlaid glass
chandelier and gasolier
English, *c*1865
Signed on the metal frame: Henry
Greene, King William St.,
London Bridge
Henry Greene was a well-
established 'lamp and lustre'
maker in the third quarter of the
19th century. He is recorded in
the City in *Kelly's Street Directory*,
and also as having another
emporium near the Pavilion in
Brighton. He was a manufacturer
of glass, china and earthenware
and patented the Bright Crown
Lamp. In 1853, when first
mentioned in *Kelly's*, the
company is Greene and Niner –
the first mention of Henry
Greene on his own is ten years
later.

The illustrated chandelier is
interesting as the upper tier of
lights appears to have been
originally intended for gas and
the lower two for candles.

707

It is not recorded who discovered gas or who first used it for illumination, but experiments with gas were going on in the seventeenth century. In 1684 the Revd John Clayton, Rector of Crofton in Yorkshire, collected quantities of gas bubbling up in a ditch in ox-bladders in which he then pricked holes and applied a flame, thus lighting the gas. During the eighteenth century various experiments had taken place with coal gas, sometimes purified and sometimes in its natural state straight from the mine. In 1765 Carlisle Spedding, a colliery manager in Cumbria, used this gas to light his offices.

John Pierre Minkelers, professor of philosophy at Louvain University, produced a form of coal gas which, in 1783, he used to light his lecture room. Philippe Lebon in 1796 produced gas by heating sawdust with which he proposed lighting part of Paris, but the idea was never taken up. George Dixon, a colliery owner, used coal gas to illuminate his house in Cockfield, Co. Durham, in the 1780s, having first experimented with an old kettle as a retort and clay pipes. In 1787 Lord Dundonald lit the whole of Culross Abbey with gas.

But it was William Murdoch who first used coal gas on a large scale for illumination. His early experiments were also done with an old kettle and a pierced thimble as a burner. In 1792 he successfully lit his house and office in Redruth, Cornwall, with gas produced in an iron retort which he built beside his house. Murdoch worked for the Birmingham firm of Boulton & Watt (see nos 330 and 333), and developed a plant to illuminate their Soho works in 1803, and the company was soon manufacturing and selling plants to other companies. Although gas lighting still produced a nasty smell, it was much cheaper than candle lighting (probably about a quarter of the cost) and it also reduced the fire risk. In 1807 a German, Frederick Albert Winsor, formed the National Light and Heat Company in London, later to become the largest gas company in the world, after being renamed the Gas Light and Coke Company in 1812. The initial costs of installing gas were, of course, expensive and meters were not used until the 1850s.

Different types of burner were evolved to produce different shapes of flame – the rat-tail produced a single large flame, the cock-spur a few smaller flames and the Cockscomb multiple small flames. In 1809 the Argand oil burner was also adapted for use with gas. In 1816 the Batswing and Fishtail burners were introduced, named for the shape of flame which they produced, which gave a brighter light than previously. In the 1850s William Sugg produced a governor-burner which kept the gas at a constant pressure and George Bray introduced flat-flame burners which appreciably increased brightness. By the 1870s gas was being produced cleanly and of consistent quality and at constant pressure.

Efforts were continually being made to improve gas lighting, particularly after early experiments with electric lighting in the 1870s, and various researchers were working on the idea of suspending a metal or chemical in the gas flame to increase

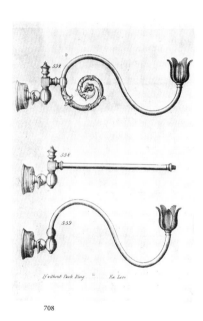

708

708 Design for gas fittings from a pattern book
English, mid-19th century
Faraday & Son

(Trustees of the Victoria & Albert Museum, London)

incandescence and produce a much brighter light. By the 1890s satisfactory incandescent mantles had been introduced in most countries, with much competition to produce an ever-improved model. The Welsbach company was making the most efficient incandescent mantles in England, and by the end of the century had produced an inverted mantle to throw light downwards from the ceiling, thus avoiding the heavy shadows formed previously by the mantles themselves.

In the early years of this century an ignition switch was invented so that gas lights could be turned on with the same ease as the new electric lights. This was done with either the use of a small pilot light or an electric element which was made to heat up and glow next to the mantle.

Most gas lamps and gasoliers have, sadly, now been converted either to electric lights or the burners replaced by candle-holders, and it is difficult to produce photographs of examples in use.

711

709

710

709 A gas lamp converted to electricity
English, *c*1885

(Trustees of the Science Museum, London)

710 A spelter lamp
Late 19th century
124cm (49in)
Converted from gas to electricity.

711 Design for a stair lamp
Alfred Stevens (1817–75)

(Trustees of the Victoria & Albert Museum, London)

217

712

713

712 A gilded bronze and glass
lantern
French, *c*1880
102cm (42in)
This would probably originally
have been fitted with an upright
gas burner.

713 A standing gasolier in brass
R.W. Winfield of Birmingham

Illustration taken from: M. Digby
Wyatt, *The Industrial Arts of the
Nineteenth Century at the Great
Exhibition, 1851*, plate 134.

714 Two gasoliers
Left: by W.R. Winfield & Sons,
right: by Messenger Sons, both of
Birmingham

Illustration taken from : J.B. Waring,
*Masterpieces of Industrial Art and
Sculpture at the International
Exhibition, 1862*, plate 246.

715 A gasolier
R.W. Winfield of Birmingham
Shown on his stand at the *Great
Exhibition of the Works of Industry
of All Nations*, 1851

714

715

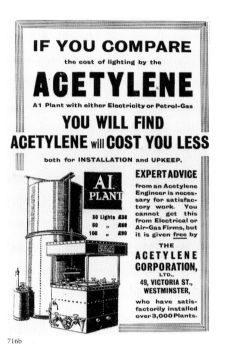

716a

716b

716c

717

718

716 Three advertisements for various forms
of household lighting
English, published *c*1914

717 Interior scene taken from a family
photograph album
English, 1880s
The Blackett family of Thorpe Lea, Windsor,
Berkshire

(Museum of English Rural Life, Reading)

718 Photograph showing part of a sitting
room
English, *c*1910
Of the two gas lights shown either side of the
chimney-glass, one has an upright burner and
the other an inverted burner.

(Museum of English Rural Life, Reading)

As the nineteenth century drew to a close, candle lighting became less and less popular. The efficiency of the oil and gas lighting and the invention of the electric light meant that it was used mainly only in poorer houses or to inject a little old-fashioned charm and atmosphere in dining rooms or at parties and receptions, where the light candles gave was much more flattering. Often a mixture of candle lighting and other forms was used.

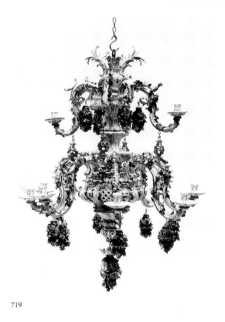

719

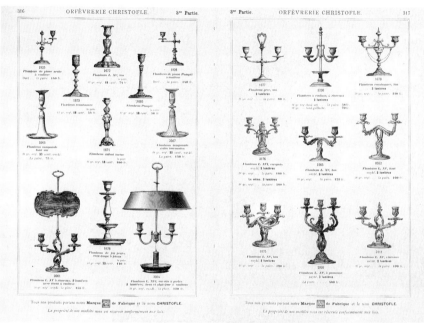

720

The door opened; they entered the hall; Emil took a candle which the porter handed to him. Before them was a fine broad staircase . . . they passed . . . into a drawing room. With the candle which he held in his hand Emil lighted two others upon the table; . . . In the uncertain light of the two feebly burning candles, Bertha could only see that a few coloured pictures were hanging on the wall.

ARTHUR SCHNITZLER, *The Spring Sonata*

721

722

719 A porcelain chandelier
Dresden, late 19th century

720 Orfèvrerie Christofle, Tarif Album
French, early 20th century
Two pages showing candle-holders in various forms and styles.

721 A porcelain candelabrum
German (Sitzendorf), late 19th century

722 A porcelain candelabrum
German (Plauen), late 19th century
57.5cm (22¾in), high

723

724

725

726

727

728

723 A silver candelabrum
London, 1899
William Hutton & Sons
61cm (24in)
Of Corinthian column form, a popular style at this period. As with most candelabra it can be used in various ways: as a candlestick (without the branches) or as a three-, four- or five-light candelabrum.

(Brand Inglis Ltd)

724 A pair of porcelain candlesticks
English (Royal Worcester), *c*1893
After models by James Hadley in Kate Greenaway style
27cm (10½in)

725 A pair of silver chamber candlesticks
French, *c*1895
20.5cm (8in) long

726 A porcelain candlestick
Scottish (Wemyss), *c*1900

727 An enamel candlestick
Limoges, *c*1875
Marked A.P., probably for A.Potier
14cm (5½in)

728 A silver and enamel candlestick
Vienna, *c*1890
Ludwig Pollitzer
19cm (7½in)
The shape is taken directly from 17th-century prototypes (see nos 39–47) but the decoration, sprays of flowers on a yellow-enamelled ground, is utterly of its period.

729 A pair of gilded bronze wall-
lights
French, 3rd quarter 19th century
66cm (26in)
In Louis XVI style and loosely
based on a pair of candelabra
made for Louis XVI's aunts, to be
used at their château de Bellevue.

730 A gilded and patinated
bronze and marble floor-standing
candelabrum
French, *c*1885
215cm (7ft)

729

730

731

731 A pair of silver candelabra on
torchères
New York, 1884
Tiffany & Co.
178.5cm (5ft 10in)
Each candelabrum for twenty
lights, the stands and candelabra
cast, raised and chased. These
candelabra and torchères are of
exceptional size, but the elaborate
acanthus and poppy decoration is
typical of much American silver
made in the last two decades of
the 19th century.
　　These impressive pieces were
made for Mary Jane Morgan, wife
of Charles Morgan, owner of
Morgan's Louisiana and Texas
Railroad and Steamship
Company. Tiffany's order
no.7846 dated 7 February 1884
records that 3,050 oz of silver
were used and that the labour
cost $7,891.

732

732 Interior of a study
Russian school, late 19th century
The room has a chandelier and a
pair of figural candelabra in the
style of the early 19th century.

733 A gilded and patinated
bronze chandelier
French, *c*1870
75cm (29½in)

734 A painted ruby glass
chandelier
Bohemian, *c*1900
112cm (44in)

735 A gilded and patinated
bronze lantern
French, *c*1910
124cm (49in)

733

734

735

One interesting nineteenth-century invention was the chimneyless lamp. With an ever-increasing export market, the fragility of the glass globes and chimneys posed a problem. The addition of a clockwork-driven fan to assist the draught provided a clear bright flame without a chimney. These were not widely used domestically because of the risk of fire from the unprotected flame.

Another improvement in efficiency was the development of the incandescent mantle, similar to those already described for gas lights. A third nineteenth-century innovation was the pressure lamp. The reservoir was pumped full of air forcing the fuel through a pre-heated tube which caused it to vaporize, igniting as it left a tiny hole at the end of the tube.

The glass chimneys and globes were made all over Europe. The best came from Saxony and Jena, but they were also made in France and Belgium and later in Britain. The chimney was a very important factor in the efficiency of a lamp as it affected the draught supply, and the height, width and location of the bulb differed from lamp to lamp. Most lamps had globe-shaped shades also in glass, sometimes decorated, and over this was sometimes put a further shade in material.

186   PUNCH, OR THE LONDON CHARIVARI.   [OCTOBER 20, 1894.

FELICITOUS QUOTATIONS.

736

736   Cartoon from the magazine *Punch* 20 October 1894
The caption reads: *Hostess (of Upper Tooting, showing new house to Friend)* 'We're very proud of this room, Mrs Hominy. Our own little upholsterer did it up just as you see it, and all our friends think it was *Liberty*!'
    Visitor (sotto voce) 'Oh, Liberty, Liberty, how many crimes are committed in thy name!'
    The shade on the standing lamp behind the hostess is similar to those shown in no.739.

A good fire was blazing in the hearth, setting great patches of golden light dancing on the ceiling and walls, illuminating the whole room with a bright and flickering radiance, against which the lamp on the table seemed but a feeble glimmer.

EMILE ZOLA, *Thérèse Raquin*, 1867

A youthful voice . . . asked him to come in. It would soon get a light, it said: but the night being wet, Mother had not thought it worth while to trim the passage lamp.

THOMAS HARDY, *Fellow-Townsmen*, 1888

737

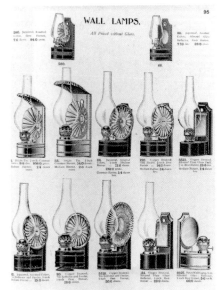

WALL LAMPS.

All Priced without Glass

738

737 An oil lamp
late 19th century

(Museum of English Rural Life, Reading)

738 S.P. Catterson & Sons Ltd, London, S.E.
1907–8 Lamp Catalogue
'Wall Lamps, All Priced without Glass'. The
lamps are priced by the dozen or gross. For
example the lamp in the centre of the middle
row is described: 'Japanned. Assorted Colors,
¾in Medium Burner . . . 11/6 dozen, 132/0
gross, Common Burner 1/4 dozen less.' The
lamp on the right of the bottom row is 'Brass
Wall Lamp, 5in Silvered Glass Reflector, 1
inch Best Burner, 5/6 each, 60/0 dozen'.

(Museum of English Rural Life, Reading)

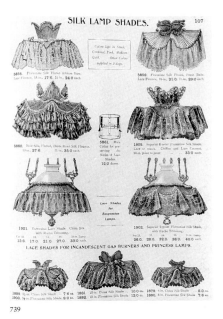

SILK LAMP SHADES.

LACE SHADES FOR INCANDESCENT GAS BURNERS AND PRINCESS LAMPS.

739

739 S.P. Catterson & Sons Ltd, London, S.E.,
1907–8 Lamp Catalogue
This page of silk lamp shades shows examples
suitable for suspension lamps and
incandescent gas burners. An 8in example in
China silk (bottom right) cost 6/-, whilst the
most expensive, at 40/- (or £2) was the 18in
version of a 'superior 9-point Florentine Silk
Shade with Ruche Trimming' (third row
right).

(Museum of English Rural Life, Reading)

740 Photograph showing a corner of a sitting
room
English, *c*1910

(Museum of English Rural Life, Reading)

741 Interior scene, taken from a family
photograph album
The Elms, Hartley Witney, Hampshire
*c*1892

(Museum of English Rural Life, Reading)

740

741

He found himself in an apartment which was simply and
neatly, though not poorly furnished; . . . From behind the
lamp on the table a female form now rose into view, that of
a young girl . . . She had been so absorbed in some
occupation on the other side of the lamp as to have barely
found time to realize her visitor's presence.

THOMAS HARDY, *Fellow-Townsmen*, 1888

My mother says that at Dursley in Gloucestershire, when
ladies and gentlemen used to go out to dinner together on
dark nights, the gentlemen pulled out the tails of their
shirts and walked before to show the way and light the
ladies. These were called 'Dursley Lanterns'.

Diary of the Revd Francis Kilvert, 10 February 1873

742 Catalogue for electroplated lamps
American, 1888
Meriden Silver Co.
Firms such as the Meriden Co. were able to make the same designs in a range of materials. These lamps were offered in copper or silver with an option of gold inlay. The firm also produced electroplate and Britannia Metal.

743 S.P. Catterson & Sons Ltd., London, S.E.,
1907–8 Lamp Catalogue
The bases are made of various materials: *top row, left to right* alabaster, bronzed iron, brass, *bottom right* electro gilt. All have Duplex burners.

(Museum of English Rural Life, Reading)

744 Catalogue for electroplated lamps
American, late 19th century
Wilcox Silver Plate Co.
A choice of finish was given for these lamps: (*left*) etched oxidized finish $13, or bright copper finish $9.50; (*right*) old silver finish $10.50, or copper finish $9.

745 Two electroplated parcel-gilt Britannia Metal oil lamps
American, *c*1890
Reed & Barton
31.5cm (12½in)

746 A parcel-gilt electroplated oil lamp
American, *c*1890
Reed & Barton
73cm (28¾in)

747 A porcelain oil lamp and reservoir, complete with substitute cover
English (Royal Worcester), shape no.1519, date code for 1892
9¾in (25in)
Fitted with Messenger's patent burner.

748 A cameo glass oil lamp
English, *c*1885
Probably Thomas Webb & Sons
41cm (16in)
Mounted with a Hinks duplex patent double burner.

749 A cameo glass oil lamp
English, *c*1885
Probably Thomas Webb & Sons
35.5cm (14in)

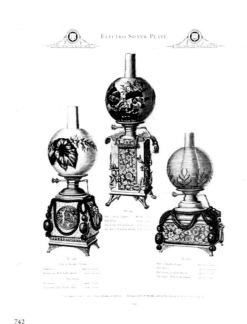

742

743

744

745

746

747

748

749

Then there were the lamp-and-candle men, at least three of them, for there was no other form of lighting, gas was despised, I forget why – vulgar, I think. They polished and scraped the wax off the candelabra, cut wicks, poured paraffin oil and unblackened glass chimneys all day long. After dark they were busy turning wicks up or down, snuffing candles, and de-waxing extinguishers . . .

LADY DIANA COOPER, writing of Belvoir in *The Rainbow Comes and Goes* (1958); quoted by Joan Evans in *The Victorians*, 1966

750

750 A pair of electroplated table oil lamps
English, early 20th century
Walker & Hall
43cm (17in)

751 A porcelain oil lamp
English (Minton), late 19th century
It is probable that the turquoise vase supported on a stretcher by the two cherubs remained in place as a decorative object in the room even during the day, when the lamp may not have been in use; the lamp was brought in, slotted into place and lit, as it became dark.

752 A porcelain lamp base
English (Royal Worcester), 1895
47cm (18½in)
Modelled after Hadley

753 Design for an oil lamp
English, early 20th century
Nelson E. Dawson
(Trustees of the Victoria & Albert Museum, London)

754 A porcelain oil lamp and reservoir
English (Royal Worcester), c1895
57in (22½in)
Fitted with a Hinks & Sons patent burner

755 A gilded metal-mounted porcelain oil lamp base
English (Royal Worcester), date code for 1903
83cm (32¾in)

756 An oil lamp, with silver base
Sheffield, 1901
Thomas Bradbury & Sons, retailed by Finnigans Ltd, Manchester
The twin burner mechanism marked: 'Hinks & Son/patent'
88cm (34¾in)

757 A glass and earthenware oil lamp
German, last quarter 19th century, with burmese glass shade
87.5cm (34½in)

751

752

753

754

755

756

757

758 The Potato Eaters
Vincent van Gogh, 1885
Lithograph, showing a peasant
family eating beneath a hanging
oil light.

759 After Dinner
Valentine Cameron Prinseps, RA
The three ladies sit reading and
knitting by the light of a simple
pressed-glass oil lamp. An unlit
candle is also on the table and a
lantern on the bench, in case it is
necessary to go out of doors.

758

760 'The Marriage of
Convenience'
*** Orchardson, 1883
The oil lamp has a shade similar
to those shown in the
advertisement, no.739.

761 The Remonstration
Alexander M. Rossi

762 S.P. Catterson & Sons Ltd.,
London, S.E.,
1907–8 Lamp Catalogue
'Suspension Lamps'.

*(Museum of English Rural Life,
Reading)*

759

760

761

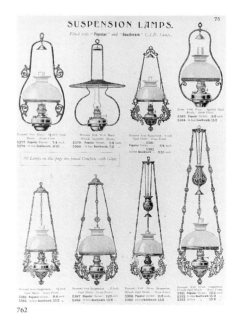

762

The potential of electricity as a source for illumination had been understood long before its practical implementation. Sir Humphry Davy had demonstrated a carbon arc-lamp as early as 1808 and Jean Foucault and Edward Staite had developed this further, but it was of little use domestically as the light it gave was far too bright.

In 1845 Edward Staite demonstrated an incandescent filament bulb in the Sunderland Atheneum. The theory behind this was simple: if a carbon filament supported between two platinum wires was sealed in a glass globe which then had an electric current passed through, the filament would become heated to such an intensity that it would glow. The main problem was creating a vacuum within the bulb, though this became possible after the invention of the mercury vacuum pump in 1865. Inventors then turned their thoughts to the best materials to use – platinum, parchmentized paper and carbonized bamboo were among others taken up and discarded with as much rapidity.

Thomas Alva Edison is credited with producing the first practicable electric light in 1879, though Sir Joseph Swan had produced a model a year earlier. Edison and Swan had acrimonious exchanges which were resolved in 1883 with the formation in England of the Edison & Swan United Electric Co. Ltd. It was just as well for them that they combined forces, as they had to fight off many competitiors with litigation to guard their patents.

To begin with electric bulbs were harshly bright, and did not have a very long life – Edison's first only lasted forty hours. But these drawbacks were soon remedied. The first house in Europe, and possibly the world, to have a complete electric light system was Cragside in Northumberland, installed by Joseph Swan himself for the owner, Sir William Armstrong, in 1880.

763 Two advertisements for electric light systems English, published early 20th century

763

763a

764 A page of electric light
fittings
Illustration taken from: Hampton
& Sons, Pall Mall East, *Designs
for Furniture and Decorations for
Complete House Furnishing*,
*c*1910.

765 Two brass electric lamps
*c*1890
Edison Patents & General
Electric Co.
35cm (13¾in) and 23cm (9in)
The nickelled brass model (right)
has an interesting swivelling light
fitting so that it can be used either
as a table lamp or wall-light.
Edison Patents socket (left) was
covered by Edison incandescent
lighting patents from 22 March
1889.

766 A picture postcard of Miss
Zena Dare
The photograph of the actress
makes no attempt to hide the
electric cable. The light switch of
the type in no.769 is on the wall
and the lamp has a shade similar
to those in no.739.

(Private collection)

767 New switches and light
bulbs
Illustration taken from: Hampton
& Sons, Pall Mall East, *Designs
for Furniture and Decorations for
Complete House Furnishing*,
*c*1910.

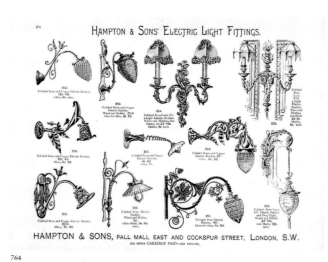

HAMPTON & SONS' ELECTRIC LIGHT FITTINGS.

HAMPTON & SONS, PALL MALL EAST AND COCKSPUR STREET, LONDON, S.W.

764

765

HAMPTON & SONS' ELECTRIC SWITCHES, LAMPS, &c.

HAMPTON & SONS, PALL MALL EAST AND COCKSPUR STREET, LONDON, S.W.

767

766

'But it's all nonsense to confuse the telephone with
electricity,' she explained. 'The telephone is something
quite apart. It is when it comes to electric light that I put
my foot down. It's all very well to point out that people in
the neighbourhood already use it, but I am deeply
suspicious of it. I wouldn't so much mind having it in a
new house – down at Lowestoft, you will remember, we
are quite up-to-date in our lighting system – but I am
afraid of a short circuit in this old St. John's Wood house.
It might set the place on fire.'

And so the study was lit by oil lamps right through the
years of my childhood, because my mother didn't trust
gas, either. There might be an unnoticed leakage, which
could suffocate us. For some reason I never discovered,
she made a distinction that certain rooms and not others
were permitted gas-light. The dining-room and the day
nursery had incandescent gas lamps, which gave a

depressing pale cold light and made a mournful singing
sound when the air got into the pipes; but we never went
to bed by anything but candlelight, and the drawing-room
– on the rare occasions when it was used – was lit by
candles.

CLARE LEIGHTON, *Tempestuous Petticoat*, London, 1948

It was a delightful experience for both of us when the
gallery was first lit up. The speed of the dynamo had not
been quite rightly adjusted to produce the strength of
current in the lamps that they required. The speed was too
fast and the current too strong. Consequently the lamps
were far above their normal brightness, but the effect was
splendid and never to be forgotten.

Letter from Joseph Swan, published in an article by John
Worsnop about Lord Armstrong in the *Newcastle Daily Journal*,
27 December 1900

768

769

768 A gilded bronze and glass
electrolier
French, *c*1910
113cm (44½in)

769 A gilded bronze chandelier
French, *c*1900
97cm (38in)

770 A pair of wall-lights
French, *c*1900

771 A gilded bronze and glass
electrolier
French, *c*1910
122cm (48in)

770

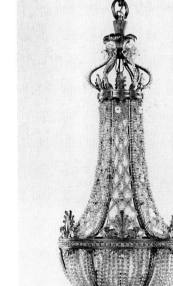

771

The electric light here is quite charming. Especially in the
bedrooms. You touch a button, and your dressing-table is
illuminated. You touch another near the *table de nuit* and
your bed is as light as day. It costs £2000 to start, and they
burn about 5cwt of coals a day in order to produce it.

I hear that Coutts Lindsay has bought five acres of
ground at Greenwich, and intends supplying all London
with electricity. It will be ever so much *cleaner*, even if it is
not cheaper than gas.

Journals and Letters of Reginald, Viscount Esher, to Lady Esher,
from Lambton Castle, 8 December 1887

Nineteenth-century writers on the decorative arts had long been horrified by the crass materialism of the series of Great Exhibitions in the second half of the century. John Ruskin and William Morris in Britain, and Léon de Laborde and Eugène-Emmanuel Viollet-le-Duc had lamented the decline in design and craftsmanship and called for a revolution in the arts. This finally occurred in the 1890s, under various names: Jugendstil, Sezessionstil, Modern Style, Arte Joren, Nieuwe Kunst, Style Liberty and Art Nouveau, a term coined in the review *L'Art Moderne* in 1881 and later used by Samuel Bing as the name for his shop in the rue de Provence in Paris (1895).

The new style rejected, as far as possible, the influence of all earlier styles and was characterized by an organic fluidity and asymmetry which lent itself particularly well to light fittings, recently given a new dimension with the invention of electricity.

772 A Loie Fuller gilded bronze lamp
French, *c*1900
Raoul Larche
33cm (13in)
The dancer Loie Fuller was the rage of Paris at the turn of the century. Though an accomplished sculptor, who produced other light fixtures as well, Larche is most famous for these gilded bronze lamps of Mlle Fuller, whose swirling draperies conceal the bulb or bulbs.

772

773 A gilded bronze and bisque porcelain lamp entitled 'Cruche Casée'
French, *c*1900
Signed: Meduat and with French foundry stamp
51cm (20in)

774 A pair of lamps, ivory set in silver bases, the heads with a crown of enamelled gold flowers studded with diamonds
*c*1900
Maker's mark J.D.
50cm (19½in)
The mark is possibly for Jean-Auguste Dampt, one of the period's most versatile mixed-media practitioners, whose most famous sculpture, 'La Fée Melusine et le Chevalier Raymondin' shows a knight in armour kissing a jewel-encrusted ivory maiden.

775 A pair of carved ivory and silver candelabra
Ivory carved by Egide Rombaux; silver: by Franz Hoosemans
Belgian, *c*1900
37cm (14½in)
Egide Rombaux, son of the sculptor Félix Rombaux, had already achieved fame for his ivory sculptures and portrait busts, before he allied with the silversmith Franz Hoosemans. Hoosemans trapped his figures in silver plant-forms to form candelabra and lamps.

776 A pair of electroplated nautilus shell lamps
*c*1900
Attributed to W.M.F.
63.5cm (25in)
The Württembergische Metallwaren Fabrik at Geislingen was formed in 1888 when the factory, founded by Daniel Straub in 1853, amalgamated with its main competitor. In 1900 the firm was employing about three thousand people and was quick to concentrate on the new Jugendstil and market its wares through sale outlets in cities such as Cologne, Vienna, Berlin and Warsaw.

773

774

775

776

777

777 A pair of electroplated candelabra
German, *c*1900
W.M.F.
27cm.(10½in)
In 1906 this design was sold for 60/- a pair in England.[121]

[121] *Art Nouveau Domestic Metalwork from Württembergische Metallwaren Fabrik, 1906*, Woodbridge, 1988

Emile Gallé, master glass craftsman, ceramicist, cabinet-maker, marqueteur and author, was the driving force behind the school of Nancy, formed in 1901. Inspired by natural forms Gallé used an unmatched battery of glass-making techniques to produce innumerable objects of a universally high quality in design and execution. Lamps constituted a major part of his glass production, from large chandeliers to small nightlights, the technique most frequently used being cameo glass. Gallé tried to oversee the entire production of about three-hundred employees, and personally designed and executed all the major pieces.

778 An intaglio-carved glass and wrought-iron lamp
French, *c*1902
Emile Gallé
81cm (32in)

778

779

780

779 A palm-leaf glass hanging
light
French, *c*1900
Emile Gallé
84.5cm (33¼in) diam

780 A cameo glass lamp
French, *c*1900
Emile Gallé
75cm (29½in)

781 A cameo glass hanging light
French, *c*1900
Emile Gallé,
38.5cm (15in) diam

782 A bronze lamp, with cameo
glass lampshade
French, *c*1900
The shade by Gallé
42.5cm (16¾in)

781

782

783 A gilded bronze and cameo
glass hanging light
French, *c*1900
Emile Gallé
77cm (30½in) across

784 A cameo glass and bronze
two-arm desk lamp
French, *c*1900
Emile Gallé
54.6cm (21½in)

785 Two cameo glass lamps
French, *c*1900
Emile Gallé
62.5cm (24½in) and
35.5cm (14in)

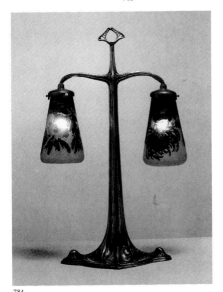

783

784

785

786

787

788

786 A bronze and glass
hanging light
French, *c*1900
70cm (27½in)

787 A gilded bronze and glass
hanging light
French (Nancy), *c*1905
Majorelle; glass: Daum
63cm (24¾in) wide

788 A bronze lamp
French (Nancy), *c*1900
Daum
38.5cm (15¼in)

789 A cameo glass and wrought-
iron lamp
French (Nancy), *c*1900
Daum
78.5cm (31in)

790 A bronze and enamelled
glass lamp
French, 1903
Daum

791 A bronze lamp
French (Nancy), *c*1900
Daum
41.5cm (16½in)

792 A cameo glass lamp
French (Lunéville), *c*1900
Muller Frères
67.75cm(6½in)
Nine of the Muller brothers and
one sister all worked at the family
glass-works in Lunéville, five of
whom had been trained in the
Gallé studio in nearby Nancy.

789

790

791

792

793

793 An iridescent glass and
gilded bronze lamp
Austrian, *c*1900
Loetz factory
54.5cm (21½in)
The Loetz factory was inherited
in 1879 by Max Ritter von Spaun,
the grandson of the founder,
Johann Loetz. It was after this
that the firm achieved
international recognition,
capturing Grand Prix at the 1889
and 1900 Paris Expositions. Very
little of their output is signed.

794 A wheel-carved cameo glass
and bronze lamp
French (Nancy), *c*1900
Largest shade signed in intaglio:
Daum/Nancy; base inscribed:
L.Majorelle/Nancy
80.2cm (31½in)
Louis Majorelle was studying
painting in Paris when, in 1879,
his father died and he was recalled
to Nancy to run the family's
furniture-making business.
Majorelle added a metal
workshop where the iron and
bronze frames for his lamps were
made. The glass was produced in
the nearby factory of the brothers
Auguste and Antonin Daum.

794

795 Design for a silver table lamp
Russian, *c*1900
Workshop of Carl Fabergé
With the St Petersburg workshop
stamp of K. Fabergé, with pencil
price R[ubles]250

(Christie's)

796 Design for a silver-gilt
mounted and jewelled table lamp
Russian, early 20th century
Workshop of Carl Fabergé

(Christie's)

795

796

On Wednesday we are all asked to
see the Museum lit up for the
Conversazione with electrical light.
Mrs Brownlow asked me yesterday
what she should wear. I told her if we
consulted our best interests, we
should all wrap our faces up in some
kind of head covering and look out
on the world with one eye. Nothing
more frightfully unbecoming than
the glare of electricity having ever
been discovered . . . (1880)

M.R. BOBBITT, *With Dearest Love to All:
Life and Letters of Lady Jebb* (1960);
quoted by Joan Evans in *The Victorians,*
1966

In the early years of this century Louis Comfort Tiffany was responsible for the production of a range of lamps and other works of art which were renowned for their exceptional design and technical virtuosity. He found the contemporary glass manufacturers in New York totally incapable of producing the effects he wanted and he began experimenting with his own company. Soon he was making the Favrile shades for which he is best known, with an amazing range of subtly blending colours and strange effects of mottling and iridescence. His floral interpretations must have appeared even more weird and wonderful in their day and were much appreciated by the Vanderbilts, the Mellons and even the White House, who were all customers.

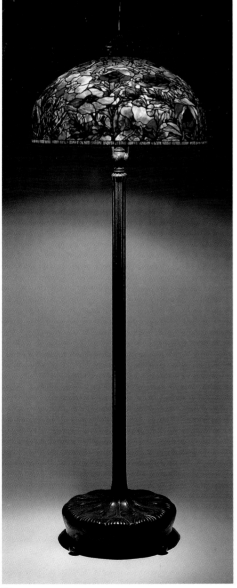

797

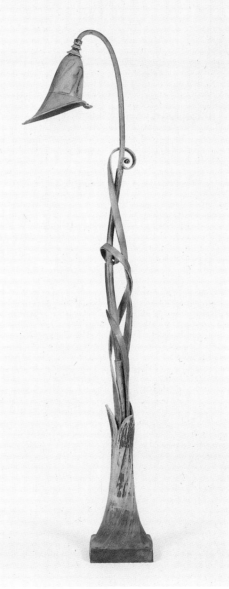

798

797 A Favrile glass and bronze lamp
American, *c*1899-1920
Tiffany
2.13m (7ft)
With 'oriental poppy' design shade.

798 A patinated bronze lamp
American, *c*1900
Tiffany
248cm (8ft 1½in)
Possibly of French manufacture and design, and imported by Tiffany.

799 A Favrile glass and bronze
'Lily' lamp
American, *c*1900–02
Tiffany
49.75cm (19½in)
Stamped with Tiffany Glass and
Decorating Company trademark,
not used after 1902.

800 A Favrile glass and bronze
lamp
American, *c*1899–1920
Tiffany
68.5cm (27in)
The shade of 'wistaria' design.

801 Three Favrile glass and
bronze lamps
American, *c*1900
Tiffany
32cm (12½in) and 30cm (11¾in)

802 A Favrile glass and bronze
lamp
American, *c*1899–1920
Tiffany
73.5cm (29in)
With 'double poinsettia' design
shade.

799

800

801

802

803

805

803 A glass and bronze lamp
American, *c*1892–1920
Tiffany
57cm (22½in)
The shade inscribed L.C.T., base
impressed on oil reserve 'Tiffany
Studios/New York/25904' and
with Tiffany Glass and
Decorating Company
monogram.

804 A Favrile glass and bronze
wall-light
American, 1899–1928
Tiffany
40cm (15¾in)

805 A bronze student's lamp
American, *c*1900
Tiffany
62cm (24½in)
Note the similarity in form to
early 19th-century Argand lamps.

806

807

808

806 A bronze 'Saxifrage' candlestick
American, *c*1899–1918
Tiffany
43.8cm (17¼in)

807 A Favrile glass and gilded bronze
counter-balance lamp
American, 1899–1920
Tiffany
37cm (14½in)

808 A Favrile glass and bronze two-arm
student lamp
American, *c*1899–1920
Tiffany
75.6cm (29¾in)

809 A silvered pewter two-light
candelabrum
Vienna, *c*1901
Designed by Joseph Maria
Olbrich, executed by Edward
Hueck
36cm (14¼in)
Joseph Olbrich was an architect
and co-founder of the Vienna
Secession with Josef Hoffman
and Koloman Moser in 1897.

810 A pair of pewter candlesticks
German, *c*1900
Kayserzinn, possibly designed by
Hugo Leven
42.5cm (16¾in)

811 A pewter candelabrum
Vienna, *c*1900
Unsigned, cast by Gerhardi
38.2cm (15in)
Gerhardi & Co. manufacturers of
pewter and other metalwork,
produced designs for Albin
Muller and J.M. Olbrich

812 A silver candelabrum
Alexander Schönauer of
Hamburg
Illustration taken from: *Journal
der Goldschmiedekunst*, Leipzig,
1909.

813 A pair of silvered bronze
candlesticks
Paris, early 20th century
Paul Follot
26cm (10¼in)
Joining Abel Landry and Maurice
Dufrère in 1901 as a designer for
La Maison Moderne, Follot
exhibited furniture and objects at
the Salon d'Automne and the
Société des Artistes Décorateurs.
He continued designing well into
the 1920s.

814 A pewter oil lamp
German, *c*1900
Kayserzinn
75cm (29½in)
J.P.Kayser founded the Kayser
Sohn pewter works in 1862 and
in 1900 his son, Engelberg
Kayser, set up a studio in Cologne
where the models for the
foundry's pewterware were
designed. Most objects were
marked Kayserzinn (ie Kayser
pewter).

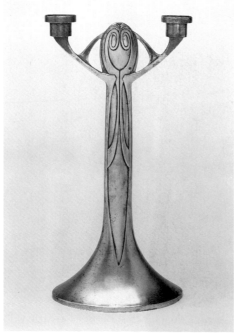

809

810

811

812

815 A painted metal chamber candlestick
*c*1880
Designed by Christopher Dresser
Perry Son & Co.
Embossed in circular plaque: 'Perry Son &
Co'; painted mark 'Dr Dresser's design Rd
No. 29466'

816 A gilded bronze candelabrum
French, *c*1900
Designed by Georges de Feure
34cm (13¼in)

817 A pair of oil lamps
French, *c*1900
Designed by Georges de Feure (1869–1928)
38cm (15in)
Dutch by birth, de Feure trained in Paris
under Joseph Chéret and was appointed head
of the design department of Samuel Bing's
Maison de l'Art Nouveau where he remained
until the outbreak of World War I.

813

814

816

815

817

818 A pair of copper and brass candlesticks
English, *c*1880
Designed by Christopher Dresser (1834–1904), probably manufactured by Chubb & Co.
32cm (12½in)
Examples of Dresser's work with Chubb & Co. during the days of the Art Furnishers' Alliance.

Dresser stressed the importance of design over craftsmanship and was strongly influenced by the art of Japan. He was manager of the Art Furnishers' Alliance 1880–83 and produced a vast quantity of designs for all kinds of household objects, many in an austere undecorated geometrical form.

819 Design for an electric light
English, early 20th century
Nelson E. Dawson

(Trustees of the Victoria & Albert Museum, London)

820 A silver candlestick
London, 1906
Designed by Reginald (Rex) Silver, for Liberty & Co.
25.5cm (10in)
Rex Silver designed for Liberty's from about 1900 onwards. Liberty never published the names of the designers in their catalogues, but Silver and Archibald Knox were chiefly responsible for designing their ranges of Cymric (silver) and Tudric (pewter) ware in Celtic style.

821 A pair of cast- and wrought-iron sconces
English, *c*1905
Designed by Ernest Gimson
36cm (14¼in)
Gimson (1864–1919), English Arts and Crafts architect and designer, set up a workshop with Ernest and Sidney Barnsley in the Cotswolds in 1895.

818

819

820

821

822 A silver and enamel chamber candlestick
Birmingham, *c*1905
Liberty & Co., designed by Archibald Knox

823 A copper and brass candlestick
English, *c*1900
W.A.S. Benson (1854–1924)
27cm (10½in)
Benson was encouraged by William Morris to set up a metal workshop in 1880. A shop was opened in Bond Street in 1887 and the firm continued until Benson's retirement in 1920.

822

823

824

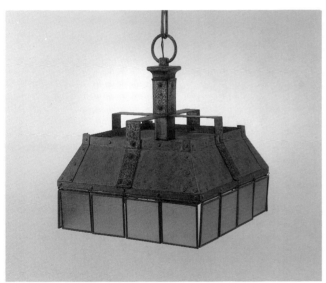

825

826

824 A hammered copper and slag glass hanging lantern
American, *c*1906
Attributed to the Shop of the Crafters at Cincinnati
33cm (13in)

825 A hammered copper wood and glass hanging light
American, *c*1910
Gustav Stickley
45.8cm (18in) wide
Gustav Stickley, trained as a stonemason, visited France and England in 1898 and returned to his native America determined to

create a new national style. In 1901 he founded *The Craftsman* magazine and enlarged his family's furniture-making company and renamed it the Craftsman Workshops. In 1915 the company was declared bankrupt.

826 An oak and leaded glass floor lamp
American, *c*1910
173cm (5ft 8in)

827

828

829

827 Two lamps from Thiébaut
Frères, Fumière & Cie, Avenue
de l'Opéra, Paris
Illustration taken from: *Les
Bronzes, l'Orfèvrerie au salon du
Mobilier*, Paris, 1905
These lamps show how popular
a debased version of Art Nouveau
had become.

828 Two lamps
From the stand of M.Camus, 50
rue Charlot
Illustration taken from: *Les
Bronzes, l'Orfèvrerie au salon du
Mobilier*, Paris, 1905.

829 Lamp in Louis XVI style
From the stand of Maison
Thiébaut Frères, Fumière & Cie,
Avenue de l'Opéra, Paris
Illustration taken from: *Les
Bronzes, l'Orfèvrerie au salon du
Mobilier*, Paris, 1905

830 Three lamps in gilded
bronze
From the stand of Emile Schmoll
Illustration taken from: *Les
Bronzes, l'Orfèvrerie au salon du
Mobilier*, Paris, 1905.

831 A vase lamp and hanging
light in the form of a fleur-de-lys
From the stand of M.E.
Mottheau
Illustration taken from: *Les
Bronzes, l'Orfèvrerie au salon du
Mobilier*, Paris, 1905.

830

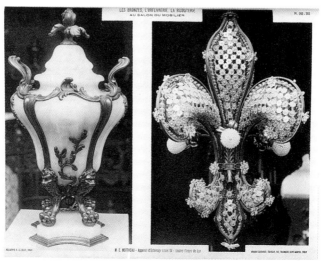

831

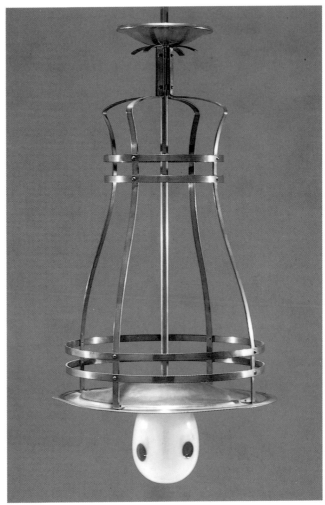

833

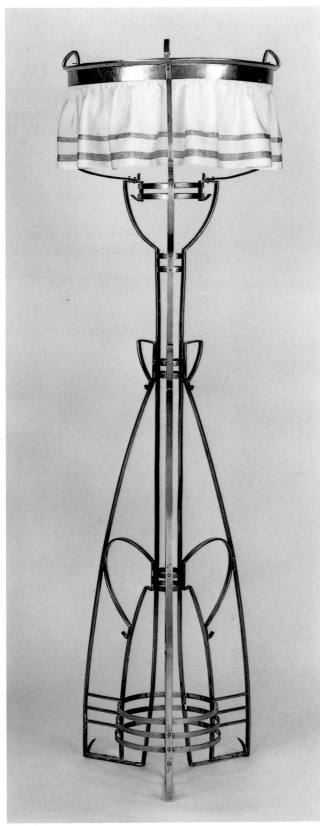

832

832 A brass standard lamp
Belgian, *c*1903–4
Gustave Serrurier-Bovy
173.5cm (5ft 8in)
Born in Liège, Gustave Serrurier-
Bovy was, along with Victor
Horta and Henry van de Velde,
one of Belgium's great
triumvirate of Art Nouveau
designers. His light fittings are
seen to best advantage in whole
rooms designed by him, and
sometimes seem awkward
without their settings.

833 A brass hanging light
Belgian, *c*1905
Gustave Serrurier-Bovy
100cm (39½in)
This light, typical of Serrurier-
Bovy, in some ways seems to pre-
shadow the Art Deco designs of
twenty years later.

Bibliography

Bascot, H. Parrott *Nineteenth Century Lighting, Candle-Powered Devices: 1783–1883,* Schiffer, Exton, PA, 1987

Caspall, John *Making Fire and Light in the Home pre 1820,* Woodbridge, 1987

de Reyniès, Nicole *Objets Domestiques,* Paris, 1987

Duncan, Alastair *Art Nouveau and Art Deco Lighting,* London, 1978

Fuhring, Peter *Design into Art, Drawings for Architecture and Ornament, The Lodewijk Houthakker Collection,* London, 1989

Eveleigh, David J. *Candle Lighting,* Shire Publications, Aylesbury, 1985

Gledhill, David *Gas Lighting,* Shire Publications, Aylesbury, 1981

Laing, A.D. *Lighting,* Victoria & Albert Museum, 1982

Mallett *Oslers: Crystal for Royalty and Rajahs,* London, 1991

Maril, Nadja *American Lighting 1840–1940,* Schiffer, Exton, PA

Meadows, Cecil A. *Discovering Oil Lamps,* Shire Publications, 1972

Michaelis, Ronald F. *Old Domestic Base Metal Candlesticks* Woodbridge, 1978

Necker, Wolf *Art Nouveau and Art Deco Lamps and Candlesticks*

O'Dea, William T. *The Social History of Lighting* London, 1958

Rushlight Club *Early Lighting, A Pictorial Guide.* Finlay Brothers, Hartford, CT, 1972

Thornton, P.K. *Seventeenth Century Interior Decoration in England, France and Holland,* Yale University Press, Newhaven, CT, 1978

Thornton, P.K. *Authentic Decor, The Domestic Interior 1620-1920,* London, 1984

834 Flint and steel used to light tapers

(Trustees of the Science Museum, London)

ILLUSTRATIONS

Unless otherwise stated in the captions to the illustrations, all photographs are from Sotheby's. A list of sale dates can be found on pp.250–52.

ACKNOWLEDGEMENTS

We have received much helpful advice and many suggestions from friends, all of whom we wish to thank. Several have generously given us their own research which, for various reasons, they were unable to publish. Among those who have been particularly generous with their time and knowledge are Dr Helen Clifford, John Culme, Peter Hornsby, Jean Schofield, Simon Spero and Eleanor Thompson.

We would also like to thank those who have written on the subject of lighting before, whose works have been of such assistance in producing this, rather different, approach to their subject:

The principal source of illustrations for the book has been auctions at Sotheby's and many colleagues there have helped us in the search for photographs. Sadly, the understandably high fees now charged for photographic reproduction prohibit the publishing of a quantity of new work. We have attempted to include as many illustrations from other sources as time and financial considerations would allow, and we are particularly grateful to those who have freely lent or given us photographs.

835 Interior with peasants
Johann Georg Trautman (1713–69)

Sale dates of objects illustrated

All sales are Sotheby's except those marked as follows:
*=Christies; **=Phillips

NUMBER	LOCATION	DATE	LOT NO
2	London	19 Feb 1987	147
3	London	19 July 1968	34
4	London	5 July 1989	190
5	New York	26 Oct 1990	144
6	Monaco	26 June 1983	320
8	London	12 Dec 1990	22
9	London	12 Dec 1990	3
10	Monaco	21 Dec 1988	618
13	New York	26 Oct 1990	164
15	London	8 Dec 1988	115
16	London	7 Dec 1989	72
17	London	12 July 1979	164, 165
18	New York	28 Nov 1980	102
20	London	1 Dec 1983	5
21	London	1 Dec 1983	42
22	London	29 March 1979	43
23	London	21 Nov 1984	431–4
27	London	9 July 1981	352
29	Monaco	21 Dec 1988	618
30	London	29 March 1979	49
33	London	30 June 1969	14
39	London	8 Dec 1983	188
40	London	13 July 1978	179
42	London	20 April 1972	67
43	Zurich	16 May 1979	46
45	London	7 April 1975	227
46	London	14 Sept 1979	146
48	London	21 Nov 1984	445
54	New York	28 Oct 1987	209
56	London	17 June 1971	126
63	London	12 Dec 1990	169
67	London	12 Dec 1990	65
68	London	11 Dec 1985	196
69	London	4 July 1969	206
71	London	6 Dec 1972	102a
72	Sussex	13/21 Sept 1988	772–7
74	London	14 Dec 1977	101
76	Mentmore	19 May 1977	682
77	Geneva	12 May 1987	124
78	London	12 Dec 1974	202
83	London	24 July 1975	204
85	London	25 Feb 1954	
86	London	9 July 1964	106
87	Geneva	14 Nov 1988	98
88	London	13 June 1983	16
89	Geneva	12 May 1987	65
90	London	17 April 1980	166
91	London	May 1990	374
93	London	7 Oct 1976	126
94	London	5 July 1989	33
97	London	10 Dec 1981	96
99	London	20 April 1972	100
101	London	8 Nov 1989	63
102	London	30 April 1987	111
103	London	3 May 1990	156
107	London	12 Feb 1981	95
108	Geneva	8 May 1989	126
111	London	24 June 1965	114
112	London	30 May 1963	41
113	London	10 July 1990	381
114	London	3 July 1980	162
116	London	15 Oct 1970	13
119	London	25 Nov 1988	42
121	New York	10 Jan 1990	408
122	London	30 June 1972	68
123	London	17 Oct 1963	751
124	London	18 May 1967	150
126	London	24 June 1988	73
127	London	8 Dec 1989	242
128	London	22 Nov 1963	17
129	London	20 June 1986	3
130	London	15 June 1990	103
131	London	20 June 1986	3
135	London	17 May 1968	35
137	London	16 Oct 1973	38
139	Geneva	14 Nov 1984	7
140	London	1 Nov 1956	76
141	London	24 Oct 1985	47, 48
142	Geneva	14 May 1990	18
145	London	4 Feb 1988	99
146	London	24 June 1988	49
147	London	24 Nov 1986	146
149	London	6 Jan 1975	67
153*	London	27 June 1973	48
155**	London	19 Feb 1991	57
156	London	24 Nov 1988	3
157	London	8 Dec 1989	246
158	London	25 Nov 1988	39
162	London	16 Oct 1989	37
163	London	17 June 1975	179
164	London	21 Nov 1990	213
165	London	14 June 1988	317
166	London	3 May 1976	140
167	Geneva	12 May 1987	32
168	London	17 Oct 1968	55
169	Geneva	8 May 1989	13
170	Geneva	12 May 1987	193
171	Sussex	21 Feb/1 Mar 1989	800
172	Geneva	11 Nov 1986	86
173	Geneva	11 Nov 1986	84
174	London	1 Nov 1990	453–5
175	London	8 Dec 1989	276
180	London	27 June 1963	99
181	London	8 June 1972	77
182	Geneva	12 Nov 1980	197
183	London	26 Feb 1976	102
184	London	25 Nov 1971	50
185	London	9 Dec 1988	81
188	London	15 June 1990	46
189	New York	8 Dec 1989	134, 135
190	London	25 Nov 1988	98
192	London	25 June 1982	106
193	London	23 May 1985	84
194	London	5 Nov 1964	147
195	London	28 June 1977	176
196	London	24 June 1988	61
197	London	5 June 1990	226
198	Sussex	15/22 Sept 1987	1398
199	London	23 May 1985	69
200*	London	19 Oct 1988	181
201	London	3 May 1990	123
202*	New York	19 April 1990	290
203	London	17 Nov 1988	102
204	Geneva	8 May 1989	128, 129
205	London	20 Oct 1966	169
206	London	24 May 1956	72
207*	London	21 Feb 1979	153
208	Geneva	13 Nov 1969	165
210	Geneva	14 May 1985	121
212	London	21 July 1966	100
213	New York	3/4 Oct 1974	91
214	London	24 April 1980	240a
215	London	25 March 1982	197
217	Geneva	12 Nov 1980	235
218	Geneva	5 May 1981	90
219	New York	24/27 Jan 1990	180
220	London	14 Nov 1968	160
221	Amsterdam	26 June 1990	241
223	London	3 April 1969	158
224	Geneva	12 May 1983	80
225	New York	5 Nov 1986	185
226	London	27 May 1988	185
227	London	8 July 1988	55
232	London	17 Oct 1963	762
234	London	12 Dec 1986	247
236	London	19 Nov 1985	103
237	Monaco	14 June 1981	148
238	London	26 June 1987	48
239	London	8 Dec 1989	63
241	London	2 Dec 1966	112
244	London	2 July 1965	131
245	London	12 Feb 1965	91
247	London	9 Dec 1988	66
248	London	24 Nov 1972	59
249	London	12 Dec 1990	3
251	London	17 Oct 1963	767
253	London	9 Dec 1988	62
255	London	25 Nov 1971	119, 120
256	London	26 June 1987	24
257	London	1 Nov 1968	63
258	Monaco	25 June 1979	60
260	London	6 Mar 1978	163
261	London	1 Mar 1990	138
263	London	3 May 1976	121
265	London	8 Dec 1977	71
267	London	12 Feb 1965	54
266	London	2 June 1977	254
267	London	12 Feb 1965	54
269*	London	19 Mar 1986	131
270	New York	2/3 Nov 1989	363
271	London	26 June 1987	25
272	London	8 Dec 1989	254
276	London	3 Dec 1964	153
277	London	8 June 1972	
278	London	3 June 1977	72
279	London	21 Feb 1989	367
280	London	26 Feb 1985	170
281	London	22 Nov 1983	73
282	London	22 Nov 1983	73a
283	London	17 June 1975	117
284	London	8 July 1966	126
285	London	22 Oct 1985	120
286	London	9 Oct 1984	219
287	London	1 July 1986	254
288	London	5 June 1990	415
289	London	25 June 1982	107
290	London	29 Sept 1987	127
292	London	24 July 1984	179
293	London	25 Nov 1985	59
295	London	17 Oct 1989	192
297	New York	17 Nov 1984	70
298	London	1 July 1986	189

299	London	6 Oct 1981	8	393	Zurich	7 May 1980	87	512	London	18 March 1982	108
300	London	1 July 1986	321	394	London	26 June 1987	64	513	London	19 Nov 1987	123
301	London	26 Feb 1985	151	395	London	25 Nov 1988	96	514	London	8 Nov 1973	179
304	Florence	27 Nov 1989	208	396	London	17 Nov 1989	16	515	London	19 July 1982	202
305	London	30 Nov 1990	168	397	London	26 June 1987	72	516	London	19 June 1981	8
306	London	22 Nov 1963	15	399	London	6 May 1980	177	519	London	25 May 1990	241–3
310	London	28 June 1963	166	400	London	17 Mar 1967	60	520	Geneva	15 May 1984	170
312	London	24 Nov 1988	28	401	London	15 July 1987	69	521	London	23 June 1967	100
313	London	24 Nov 1988	34	402	London	21 Nov 1984	437, 438	522	London	5 Feb 1987	152
314	London	24 May 1985	115	403	London	18 Oct 1973	194	523	London	30 Nov 1990	194
315	London	19 June 1981	6	404	Sussex	9 Dec 1986	700	524	London	21 Nov 1990	213
320**	London	19 Feb 1991	130	405	Geneva	12 Nov 1985	71	525	London	5 Nov 1987	72
321	London	17 April 1964	25	406	London	18 Oct 1988	535	526	London	24 June 1988	16
322	Monaco	25 Nov 1979	151	407	London	3 Feb 1976	6	527	London	8 Dec 1989	373
323	London	24 Nov 1988	31	408	London	20 Nov 1987	189	528	New York	26 Oct 1990	285
325	London	20 April 1972	158A	409	London	20 Nov 1987	190	529	London	25 Nov 1988	148
326	London	22 May 1972	22	410	London	20 Nov 1987	191	535	Geneva	15 Nov 1988	78
327	London	20 June 1988	298	411	London	16 Oct 1990	169	536	London	26 June 1987	119
328	London	17 Nov 1989	12	412	London	4 May 1990	30	537	London	5 July 1985	205
330	London	18 Feb 1972	109	414	Belgravia	8 Mar 1979	203	539	New York	26 Oct 1990	48
331	London	1 Nov 1963	28	415	London	6 Mar 1987	337	542	New York	26 Oct 1990	34
333	London	28 Mar 1968	155	416	London	5 July 1989	190	543	London	16 Nov 1990	203
336	London	10 July 1990	321	417	Sussex	9 Dec 1986	781	544	London	22 Nov 1984	195
337	London	15 June 1990	71	422	London	17 Oct 1988	85	545	London	3 June 1977	75
339	London	15 June 1990	55	424	London	22 Nov 1988	58	546	New York	21 Jan 1983	212
340	London	15 June 1990	56	425	London	9 May 1974	81	548	London	24 June 1988	6
341	London	24 Nov 1988	26	426	Florence	27 Nov 1989	120	549	London	8 Dec 1989	385
342	London	24 May 1985	114	427	Monaco	21 June 1986	322	550	London	24 Nov 1988	36
344	Monaco	27 Nov 1979	824	428	Florence	27 Nov 1989	141	558	London	27 April 1989	750
345*	New York	27 Oct 1986	589	429	Sussex	6 Feb 1990	863	559	London	27 May 1988	254
346	Monaco	14 June 1981	75	430	London	3 Feb 1976	26	560	Geneva	14 Nov 1988	108
348	Monaco	22 Feb 1986	175	434	London	22 Oct 1973	54–6	561	Vienna	23 Mar 1989	27
349*	London	25 Oct 1989	174	437	London	10 July 1986	173	562	Vienna	23 Feb 1989	21
350	London	23 Oct 1958	117	441	London	26 May 1989	181	563	New York	26 Oct 1990	282
351	London	30 Nov 1978	104	442	London	9 Dec 1988	214	565	London	9 June 1989	232
352	London	16 Oct 1975	172	449	London	7 July 1989	1	571	London	7 July 1989	14
353	Monaco	26 Nov 1979	609	450	New York	26 Oct 1990	124	572	London	16 June 1990	131
354	London	15 June 1990	69	453	London	16 Nov 1990	236	573	London	12 Feb 1988	3
355	London	30 Nov 1990	154	454	London	21 June 1988	8	575	New York	22 Oct 1988	176
356	London	26 June 1987	79	455	London	22 May 1986	317	576	London	16 June 1989	166
357	London	8 Dec 1989	294	456	Vienna	23 Feb 1989	47	581	London	27 April 1989	782
358	London	24 Nov 1989	84	457	London	16 June 1989	140	582	London	26 May 1989	240
359	London	24 Nov 1988	32	462	New York	26 Jan 1990	1015	583**	London	27 Nov 1990	164
360	London	15 June 1990	80	464	London	27 Nov 1986	601	584	London	19 June 1981	146
361	London	15 June 1990	66	466	London	5 July 1985	205	590	London	15 Nov 1990	30
362	Quenby	25 Oct 1972	986	467	London	26 June 1987	115	591	London	30 Nov 1990	241
363	London	1 Nov 1963	67	468	London	16 June 1989	139	594	London	9 Dec 1988	192
365	London	23 Feb 1990	15	472	Sussex	23 Feb 1988	596	596	London	20 June 1986	104
369	Monaco	14 June 1982	571	477	New York	21 Jan 1983	203	597	London	3 May 1990	16
370	London	12 Feb 1988	9	480	Tyninghame	29 Sept 1987	112	598	Sussex	15 July 1986	1548
371	London	8 Dec 1989	296	482	London	30 Mar 1973	109	600	London	23 Jan 1964	19
372	London	7 July 1989	15	484	Sussex	19 Sept 1989	697	602*	London	13 April 1989	19
373	London	30 Nov 1990	237	487	London	15 Mar 1988	7	605	London	15 Nov 1990	38
376	London	24 May 1985	123	488	Sussex	20 June 1989	1631	608	London	28 Jan 1965	37
377	London	24 May 1985	123	492	New York	6 Feb 1980	558	611	London	24 Sep 1977	28
379	London	30 June 1981	184	494	London	30 Nov 1990	172	613	London	16 July 1970	128
380	London	4 March 1986	157	495	London	24 June 1988	22	615	London	15 Nov 1990	37
381	Geneva	8 May 1989	122	496	Geneva	13 Nov 1989	44	616	London	17 Oct 1985	456
382	London	5 April 1963		498	London	26 June 1987	155	617	New York	5 Nov 1986	102
383	London	22 Nov 1963	111	499	Zurich	18 Nov 1977	155	619	London	27 May 1988	274
384	London	15 June 1973	45	500	London	20 Oct 1981	173	620	London	27 May 1988	275
385	London	4 July 1989	216	501	London	19 June 1969	83	621	London	27 May 1988	276
386	London	23 Jan 1969	61	502	London	15 Oct 1970	65	622*	London	20 May 1987	134
387	Amsterdam	26 June 1990	123	505	London	14 Nov 1975	27	623	London	21 Oct 1986	370
388	Geneva	11 Nov 1986	114	507	London	23 May 1985	142	624	London	18 June 1987	439
389	New York	3 Oct 1974	152	509	London	18 July 1968	121	627	London	17 Nov 1989	156
392	London	4 Feb 1988	38	510	London	24 April 1969	210	628	London	3 Nov 1989	431

631	London	3 Nov 1989	441
632	London	18 March 1988	260
633	London	29 Nov 1985	87
634	London	6 Nov 1986	515
635	London	15 June 1990	126
636	London	3 Nov 1989	448
638	Belgravia	9 June 1977	602
639	London	22 May 1984	254
640	London	27 April 1989	134, 135
641	Belgravia	9 June 1977	395, 396
644	Belgravia	26 July 1973	237
645	Belgravia	20 July 1972	190
646	London	24 July 1984	230
649	London	22 Nov 1989	280
650	Belgravia	19 Feb 1981	432
651	New York	17 Nov 1990	112
652	Belgravia	6 March 1980	286
653	London	13 July 1987	130
654	Belgravia	10 April 1980	298
655	Belgravia	10 Dec 1976	491
656	London	17 July 1990	461
657	Belgravia	19 Dec 1976	469
659	London	27 April 1989	784
664	London	2 Nov 1989	141
665	London	2 Nov 1989	142
667	London	21 March 1989	282
679	London	3 Nov 1989	468
681	London	27 Nov 1969	197
684	London	15 Nov 1988	331
686	London	22 Aug 1988	7
689	Belgravia	6 Dec 1973	33
691	New York	15 Dec 1981	55
693	London	17 Nov 1988	18
695	Belgravia	20 Feb 1975	102
696**	London	26 Jan 1990	193
697	Belgravia	21 July 1976	44
698	Belgravia	21 July 1976	43
699	London	23 June 1987	539
700	London	23 June 1987	633
701	London	10 Feb 1977	59
702	Sussex	8 Nov 1989	3116
703	Sussex	2 Nov 1989	1493
704	New York	26 Oct 1990	123
706	London	18 March 1988	215
707	London	18 March 1988	199
710	Sussex	28 Jan 1988	535
712	London	3 Nov 1989	526
719	London	5 Nov 1987	77
721	London	5 Nov 1987	75
722	Sussex	24 July 1989	1402a
724	London	19 Dec 1989	148
725	Belgravia	14 Dec 1978	154
726	Gleneagles	31 Aug 1987	208
727	London	13 July 1978	81
728	Belgravia	15 Sept 1977	4
729	London	18 March 1984	159
730	London	9 June 1989	185
731	New York	24 June 1987	83
733	London	3 Nov 1989	458
734	London	3 Nov 1989	382
735	London	3 Nov 1989	530
745	Belgravia	9 June 1977	362, 363
746	Belgravia	29 Mar 1973	22
747	London	22 Feb 1983	186
748	Belgravia	22 Nov 1973	195

749	Belgravia	22 Nov 1973	198
750	Belgravia	10 May 1979	55
751	London	23 June 1987	570
752	Sussex	18 April 1989	1129
754	London	15 Mar 1988	268
755	London	29 Sept 1987	305
756	Belgravia	3 Nov 1977	185
757	Belgravia	24 July 1975	221
758	London	26 June 1990	407
759	London	17 Dec 1986	155
761	Sussex	27 Jan 1987	2893
765	London	5 Oct 1990	350, 351
768	London	3 Nov 1989	538
769	London	9 June 1989	221
771	London	9 June 1989	128
772	London	23 June 1989	296
773	Sussex	16 May 1989	514
774	New York	17 June 1989	637
775	New York	20 June 1986	
776	London	3 Mar 1989	168
777	London	23 June 1989	185
778	New York	1 Dec 1989	596
779	Monaco	4 Dec 1988	20
780	Monaco	24 Oct 1982	25
781	Monaco	25 June 1981	20
782	London	4 June 1987	31
783	Monaco	19 Oct 1986	94
784	New York	20 Nov 1987	458
785	London	7 Oct 1982	23, 24
786	Monaco	15 Oct 1989	223
787	London	17 June 1988	114
788	Monaco	15 Oct 1989	106
789	New York	7 Dec 1985	114
790	Monaco	11 Oct 1987	90
791	Monaco	11 Oct 1987	90
792	London	13 April 1984	4
793	London	3 Mar 1989	6
794	New York	1 Dec 1989	584
795*	London	27 April 1989	462
796*	London	27 April 1989	471
797	New York	17 Nov 1984	276
798	London	29 Nov 1984	5
799	London	20 Oct 1989	43
800	New York	1 Dec 1989	893
801	Monaco	17 April 1988	15–17
802	New York	8 June 1988	447
803	New York	1 Dec 1989	913
804	New York	1 Dec 1989	919
805	London	16 May 1986	242
806	New York	1 Dec 1989	376
807	New York	19 Mar 1988	288
808	New York	19 Mar 1988	290
809	London	20 Oct 1989	172
810	London	19 Dec 1986	498
811	New York	17 Nov 1988	514
813	Monaco	5 April 1987	202
814	Monaco	11 Mar 1984	337
815	London	3 Nov 1983	43
816	London	3 Mar 1989	169
817	Monaco	11 Mar 1984	338
818	London	4 Dec 1985	76
820	London	16 May 1986	377
821	New York	17 May 1985	457
822	London	29 Nov 1984	185
823	Sussex	15 July 1986	1236

824	New York	10 Mar 1989	534
825	New York	23 Feb 1985	63
826	New York	16 June 1989	89
832	Monaco	6 Oct 1985	210
833	Monaco	15 Oct 1989	227

836 Striking a flint

(Trustees of the Science Museum, London)

Index

837 A working model of a
candle-moulding machine
English, *c*1888
Price's Patent Candle Co.

*(Trustees of the Science Museum,
London)*